HOW TO YOURSELF I AND HAPPY

C000030464

Quickly Discover the Many Proven Benefits of Walking for a Healthy Body & Mind

by

RUSS WILLIAMS

TABLE OF CONTENTS

It is an undisputable medical fact that walking regularly does have significant health benefits and there really is no shortage of medical and scientific research to back up this claim.

If you want to get fitter, increase your lower body strength, maintain your balance, lose weight, control cholesterol and high blood pressure and a lot more besides then you really should consider adding walking to your fitness routine.

It could be a short walk to your local shop right the way through to a much longer walk with family and friends or in my case normally a four-legged friend.

Walking *will* help you burn calories and lose weight, control high blood pressure and even manage any elevated Cholesterol levels that you may have and that is just for starters.

I know some people sneer at walking. Why go to the Gym to get on a treadmill at 5mph say the naysayers? What's the point?

In March of 2020, the *Journal of the American Medical Association* released findings of a major new survey on the effects of walking on people over 40 years of age.

They found that the more steps a person took the less chance they had of dying prematurely. Of course, certain criteria were taken into account like age, smoking, sex, health and education.

The findings were compelling.

4860 people took part in the survey and were each given a tracker to count their steps per day.

They found over-40s could take just 8,000 steps a day to lower the risk of death from cardiovascular diseases and cancer by 50%.

By increasing the number of steps from 4,000 to 8,000, researchers concluded that the middle-aged lower their risk of death also by 50%.

Step monitoring in more than 4,800 adults aged 40 or over implies that higher step counts lower the chance of death from any cause over a 10-year period.

Taking 12,000 steps a day lowers the risk by 65 percent, while taking just 2,000 steps increases the risk of death by 50 percent.

Of the 4,840 participants, each took an average 9,124 steps a day.

So, as it turns out if you currently do not walk regularly you are missing out on the proven benefits of exercise walking as an extremely effective physical activity whether you do it outdoors or indoors.

"Walking can be as good a workout, if not better, than running" according to **Dr Matt Tannenberg**, CSCS, a sports Chiropractor and Certified Strength and Conditioning Specialist in the US.

John Ford a certified exercise physiologist points this out "While I would love to say that walking can be just as effective as a workout, I'm not going to lie to you. In fairness the two shouldn't be compared against each other".

"Running, due to larger muscle recruitment, greater forces exerted and fast motion capability, will always have the leg up on walking".

He's right, walking may not be a better work out, but it certainly IS a better exercise choice for many people.

Walking is a great form of exercise too and is really effective in helping people reach their desired fitness goals and losing weight.

A lot of medical professionals recommend walking as their suggested workout over running because of its numerous benefits.

There have been comparison studies undertaken to compare the medical benefits for runner's vs walker's and for people who were brisk walkers they had similar results to the runners over a 6-year period.

Pretty prominent health markers were achieved by people walking at a moderate intensity and boosted and protected their health just as well as running.

Great news for those of us who are filled with dread at the prospect of going for a jog!

This book will *explain* the many physical and mental improvements that are derived from regular walking, show you the various types of walking that you can do based entirely on your level of fitness and provide you with all the proof that you need to actually get some walking shoes on and get out there to getter fitter and mentally happier.

My name is *Russ Williams* and for the last 36 years I have been a broadcaster, journalist and occasional author and now I am a serial walker and have never felt better.

The irony is that I spent a huge amount of my career time at work in the most sedentary state possible sitting in studios or just sat staring at a computer screen.

I played the occasional round of golf and did the odd bit of gardening and never entertained the idea of joining a Gym which I see, rightly or wrongly, as tedious places full of over competitive types who were out to intimidate me physically.

Around 15 years ago I had a dog called Daisy a sprightly Staffordshire Bull terrier who was able to enjoy a large garden to play in but was clearly keen for 'walks'.

That was when I decided that my responsibility to the dog meant that I too had to start going for regular 'Walkies'.

This we did on a regular basis until she sadly died just over 6 years ago from cancer and partial blindness. The day I had to say goodbye to her remains one of the saddest days of my life.

Almost as a tribute to her and our bonding time together for months after her passing I kept walking the same routes that we had done so regularly.

I found it comforting and in a strange kind of way often felt her presence. It was enormously comforting.

After a while I realized that my body needed to walk and craved the benefits that I have briefly touched on already.

I remember having my blood pressure taken by a nurse at my doctor's surgery and she said it was borderline hypertension - the area of the BP scale that the medical profession considers a holding area to full blown high blood pressure.

The nurse said if I could do half an hour's moderate exercise 3 times a week it would probably lower my blood pressure provided, I wasn't eating a diet of fast food, drinking large volumes of alcohol and didn't smoke.

Well, fast food wasn't really my scene. I did enjoy a few beers but nothing over the top and fortunately for my alcohol intake I loathe the taste of spirits.

The Elephant in the nurses' room was smoking. I knew it was wrong, but I strangely enjoyed it and I was addicted. Don't get me wrong I wasn't a 20 a day merchant but smoking seemed part of my very being.

So, I decided to take up walking with Daisy and whilst heeding most of the nurse's advice carried on enjoying tobacco.

My mindset was if I do some regular exercise then my health would be improved if not saved by the 'everything in moderation' mantra.

Sure enough I burnt off a little fat and my blood pressure did drop to acceptable levels for my age. I could breathe easier, I felt fitter and walking almost became like a must have drug for my body and its welfare.

That was 15 years ago and even though I no longer have Daisy's love and companionship to encourage me I do have a very fit and demanding Staffordshire Bull terrier called Lottie whose physical demands are even more considerable.

Before Lottie it was just a walk for all the right reasons but with her in my life, I had to up my game to the further benefit of my health.

We had to walk faster and for longer and over fields and through forests – Lottie is high-energy and inquisitive, she thinks paths are boring!

Today a typical week would see us walk around 25 to 28 miles a week together. We have one complete day off and another day is almost like a warm down day in the same way a footballer warms down after a match or after training.

Lottie would walk forever 7 days a week because she is a typical Staffie. Relentless.

I call her my Gym.

A typical walking week for us would be say 28 miles which equates to 1345 miles a year – not far off twice the length of the UK.

Trust me, I am not giving you these figures to boast or intimidate or scare you.

Far from it, because I promise you that once you start walking regularly you will be amazed at how far you actually walk with comparatively little effort!

I have researched walking and want to share with you everything that I think will help you *whatever your age* or level of fitness.

Walking IS the 'Superfood' of fitness.

The more you do it the bigger the benefits will get

I walk in rain, sleet, snow, wind or sun. Cold or hot weather. It's an activity that is satisfying, rewarding and benefits not only me but little Lottie too.

It's a win-win situation. I really do walk the walk and, in this book, I will *talk the walk* to you and explain why it's a simple activity that can offer *so* many physical and mental benefits and best of all it's completely free to do!

WHERE TO GO WALKING:

The good news is the possibilities are endless.

Parks, cities, heritage trails, canal towpaths, forests, fields, towns, riverside paths, national parks, beaches, woodlands, heaths, nature reserves, even your local Gym…the list goes on and on.

The only golden rule is that you should always check that where you want to walk is permissible – this certainly applies to walking in the countryside.

Public footpaths are exactly what it says on the tin, but many landowners will not take kindly to somebody who deliberately diverts from paths or designated walkways/ bridleways to walk on private land. Always try and stay within the rules and be respectful.

In the world there are so many places where you will have a right to roam, it's just about staying within the parameters of where walking is allowed.

From walking football, basketball and rugby to becoming a member of the Ramblers there really are so many ways to get out there walking, enjoying life and feeling healthier and fitter,

THE BENEFITS OF WALKING ON YOUR BODY

Let's start how I mean to carry on with our first piece of good news.

There are more people who don't like to go to the Gym than those who do.

These are the people who don't like to work out BUT they actually DO every day by walking going about their daily business.

Every time that you take a walk you are doing aerobic exercise!

Billions of people around the world walk every day and I would like to bet you that most do not think of their 'walk' as aerobic activity.

Walking is not hard to do, and it gives you more health benefits than sporadic heavy exercising.

It will help you feel good and look good too!

Exercise does not have to be harsh and difficult. A simple brisk walk each day can greatly improve your health.

You have many options for the type of walking that you can do, and they will be revealed later on in this book.

Grab your smartphone and headphones, listen to your favourite Spotify playlist and get walking for better physical and mental health!

Let's start with a look at the many *proven* specific health benefits of walking for you and your body and some of them may surprise you…

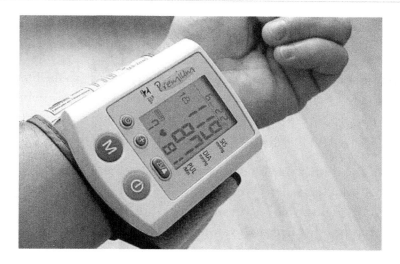

LOWERS BLOOD PRESSURE:

Walking is a great way of lowering or controlling your blood pressure but before I go into detail on how much you will have to do to get results, it's important to understand the mechanics of the body.

Having high blood pressure levels and not doing enough exercise are closely related but small changes such as walking regularly can really make a BIG difference.

So why are high blood pressure and exercise related?

If you commit to regular physical activity, it will naturally make your heart stronger.

A stronger heart can pump more blood around the body with far less effort than for somebody who does little or no exercise.

If your heart, because of exercise, is stronger it will pump blood around the body far more easily, decreasing the force on your arteries, resulting in lower blood pressure.

The top number in a blood pressure reading is called 'systolic' blood pressure and this is the figure that you doctor would really look at.

The bottom number is called 'diastolic' – is the resistance to the blood flow in the blood vessels and the general medical view is that acceptable blood pressure would give a reading of 120/80 – but don't panic if you are slightly higher than this reading.

However, the truth is that blood pressure increases and decreases naturally over a 24-hour period and this is the reason that if somebody gives consistently 'higher' blood pressure they are usually put on a blood pressure monitor by their doctor for at least 24 hours.

The spikes and troughs in blood pressure readings can be interpreted by getting an average figure of top and bottom blood pressure figures over the same period.

Becoming more active by walking can lower the top figure by an average of 4 to 9 millimetres of Mercury (mm HG) which is actually as good as some blood pressure medications.

Some people reluctantly accept medication for treating high blood pressure levels and would do pretty much anything to not have to take them on a regular basis.

You have the opportunity to really lower your blood pressure and be drug free in achieving that goal.

Walking can not only help lower blood pressure, but it can also prevent it rising as you age.

It is generally accepted that to keep your blood pressure low by walking, you have to exercise on a regular basis – a minimum of 30 -40 minutes walking 3-5 times a week – although taking some exercise everyday would be the best solution.

It's worth investing in a blood pressure monitor and taking your levels 3 times a day at roughly the same time.

Be aware that if you take your blood pressure reading on returning from a walk your levels will be higher as you've just done 30-40 minutes of aerobic walking exercise.

Take your reading again after 5-10 minutes and it should be much lower.

Make a note of each reading including your pulse rate if your chosen monitor has that facility and after a few days you should be able to see your blood pressure pattern.

To have blood pressure at 'hypertensive' levels would give a reading of 150/90 and pre-hypertension often a pre-cursor to high blood pressure begins at a level of 140/90.

As you start walking regularly you should see figures start to lower both at the top and bottom of the blood pressure scale. When that starts to happen, you will feel a real sense of achievement!

But remember, the benefits will only last as long as you regularly exercise, and it will take around anywhere between one and three months for regular walking to have an impact on your blood pressure levels.

Regular walking is a proven way of lowering blood pressure levels and maintaining healthy levels but in my experience not everyone can spare 40 minutes 5 days a week to exercise.

Busy lifestyles, work commitments and family time often cloud the commitment.

One way around this is to walk briskly for 4 10minute burst throughout the day or evening.

Or you could take a regular faster walk in your lunch hour – where there's a will there is a way. No excuses.

As long as you get your heart rate up and could hold a conversation whilst walking and not be able to sing then this is the level of exercise for the best results.

A friend of mine who is a retired GP always maintained that a light sweat was also a good indicator that the exercise was having a beneficial effect on the body – in this case lowering blood pressure.

Finally, Hydration is something to be aware of particularly if you do brisk walks or live in a warm climate.

It is important to stay hydrated.

Becoming dehydrated will affect your blood pressure and can worsen your condition.

Drink a cup of water before every walk and an additional cup of water for each mile that you walk, at a modest pace that will be approximately every 20 minutes.

The general recommendation is to let thirst be your guide. However, if you are on medication this may be normal for you

A good idea is to carry a water bottle on your walk so you can have access to water whenever you wish as you walk.

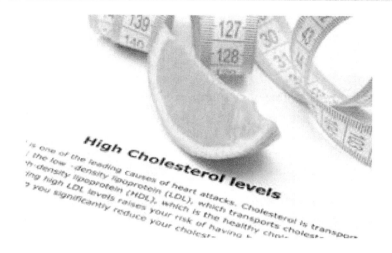

High Cholesterol levels

...is one of the leading causes of heart attacks. Cholesterol is transpor...
...the low-density lipoprotein (LDL), which is the healthy choles...
...h-density lipoprotein (HDL), which transports choles...
...ing high LDL levels raises your risk of having h...
...? you significantly reduce your cholest...

CONTROL CHOLESTEROL LEVELS:

Cholesterol is a waxy substance needed to make healthy cells but having too much of it causes a build-up in the blood vessels, which blocks oxygen from flowing through arteries to the rest of the body.

Healthy levels are essential to your body working the way it should in the correct way.

There are, as you may be aware, 2 types of cholesterol.

Low-Density Lipoprotein (LDL) or Bad Cholesterol and High-Density Lipoprotein (HDL) or Good Cholesterol.

LDL cholesterol is the type that can cause the body problems as it is responsible for the formation of plaque in the arteries which can lead to serious cardiovascular issues.

HDL cholesterol in essence eats the bad cholesterol.

Debate has raged about statins and their use for controlling cholesterol.

Most doctors swear by them as an effective treatment, but a significant number of the medical profession are questioning their overuse and its validity.

However, almost all agree that statins are of significant help for anyone who has had a 'cardiac event'.

I'm guessing that if you have elevated cholesterol levels you would be interested in the benefits of walking to control them to healthy levels.

We all need cholesterol it's a crucial element of the human body – the brain for example thrives on cholesterol.

Cholesterol in our bloodstream travels to the liver where it gets filtered out of the body.

Regular walking can address high cholesterol levels and indeed there is some evidence that LDL levels can come down particularly with slower walking rather than a fast-brisk walk.

Either way both these different speeds of walking are proven to reduce the levels of cholesterol in your blood – LDL levels come down and HDL levels increase especially with faster walkers.

You won't find a medical practitioner on the planet who will complain about LDL coming down and HDL rising.

What's interesting is researchers are still trying to determine *exactly* how exercise affects your cholesterol levels.

But the bottom line is clear: moderate exercise appears to have favourable effects on your cholesterol levels.

Moderate walking exercise has reduced LDL cholesterol levels by up to 10% in a few studies.

Others have had slightly more negligible results but as far as HDL or 'good cholesterol' is concerned exercising this way regularly shows a typical increase of anywhere between 3 and 6 percent.

Although this may not seem like much, combining exercise with other lifestyle changes like stopping smoking, losing weight and diet changes can help keep your cholesterol levels, as well as the rest of your body, healthy.

Doctors agree that having lower blood pressure and lower 'Bad' cholesterol levels significantly reduces your chances of having a heart attack or stroke.

DIABETES AND WALKING:

Walking is very beneficial for people with Diabetes.

Some recent studies suggest regular exercise like walking can reduce risk of diabetes by up to 60%.

For anyone starting out on a walking program who is a diabetic seeking the advice of a medical professional before they start is sensible.

Don't try and go from zero walking exercise to 30 to 60 minutes a day from scratch.

Everything has to be measured but once you get going the benefits for a diabetes sufferer are significant.

By walking for just 30 minutes to 45 minutes a day a diabetic person will achieve improved glucose control.

Exercise sees the muscles absorb blood sugar which prevent it from building up in the bloodstream.

Depending on the individual this effect can last from hours through to days but it's important to point out that the reduction in blood sugar levels is not permanent.

This is why REGULAR walking is so important for the control of blood glucose levels.

Another benefit of walking is improved cardiovascular fitness, a really important benefit for diabetics who are at increased risk from heart disease.

Walking is fantastic for helping weight control as it burns calories, helping control weight and reducing overall health risks.

The health benefits of walking begin to become real at just 30 minutes a day of walking exercise.

You don't have to push yourself physically and can start at a slow pace and gradually quicken over time as you feel your fitness levels rise.

As each week goes by increase your walking time by 5 or 10 minutes until you reach what is regarded as the optimum length of walking time for a person with diabetes – 45 to 60 minutes a day 5 or 6 days a week.

That's an ideal amount of time for blood glucose maintenance.

Incidentally, blood glucose levels start to change positively around 30 minutes a day of walking.

Be aware that seeing the results that you desire can take time.

Being consistent in your walking exercise is important and a good idea is to set yourself reasonable, achievable goals to increase your fitness levels.

The activity of walking is paramount but so is resting enough, letting your body fully recover and making sure that you are having good nutrition by eating healthily.

Keep your walking regime balanced. Don't do a couple of hard days in a row because probably your body will tell you that it doesn't like it.

Eating correctly before and after your walks is also paramount.

A diabetic has to be very aware before snacking of the type of food needed when walking.

This will entirely depend on when they last ate, what is happening with blood sugar levels and how hungry they feel.

You will find that your nutritional needs will be dictated by the length of the walk and the pace that you walk at.

A walk of an hour at a fast pace means that you should think carefully about eating something during your walk.

If you take medication for lowering your blood sugar levels – Sulphonylureas – always check your blood sugar levels before you set off walking.

This also applies to somebody who has Type 1 Diabetes.

During the walk itself blood sugar levels should also be checked and again at the end of the walk because the exercise may cause a drop in blood sugar level.

Most diabetics would carry Hypo treatments so that they can be used if blood glucose levels fall below 4mmol/l.

Blood sugar levels spike around 90 minutes after eating so this is something to be aware of.

If in any doubt a doctor will be able to give you advice on when to check your blood sugar levels for your regular walking program.

Many people who suffer with diabetes embrace walking as a way of controlling glucose levels.

Always take your diabetes I.D or bracelet with you, tell someone the route that you plan to take and taking a mobile phone with you would be sensible.

Something that I will cover later in the book is footwear and foot health for walking, but it is a particularly important for somebody who has diabetes.

One of the symptoms of diabetes is a numbness in the foot which means that cuts, abrasions and blisters are hard to detect.

These types of minor injuries are often slow to heal and often are prone to infection because a typical diabetes sufferer has reduced blood flow in the small blood vessels in the extremities of the body.

If you develop a foot condition stop walking regularly until you have had the injuries looked at by a professional podiatrist or your doctor.

Always listen to your body, prepare before your walk to ensure that you get the full benefits of walking with diabetes safely.

IMPROVE YOUR POSTURE:

If you look at a lot of people, they tend to stand or sit with a hunch.

Hours of working at a computer for example plays havoc with the bodies posture. Bad posture gives the body problems like persistent back aches for example.

Posture is very important, and walking is a very good way of improving it with a few additional benefits as well.

For a good walking posture, you should make sure that your head is UP and looking forward when you walk.

Try and keep your back as straight as you can by slightly tightening your abdominal muscles. To know for sure if your back really is straight always aim for creating a space between your ears and shoulders.

You should feel that your neck, shoulders and back feel relaxed at all times.

Swing your arms naturally with a slight bend.

A combination of these two things will help your shoulders naturally rotate and work your abdominal muscles.

Swinging your arms (backwards and forwards as you walk) faster not only increases your speed but also tones your arms, shoulders and upper back.

Avoid looking down at the ground or hunching over with your shoulders and back as you walk.

Make sure that your chin is up and look straight ahead in front of you instead of down.

Keep your body core tight and your shoulders down and back. This position helps to strength your muscles, allowing you to have good posture all day long.

By paying just a little attention and thinking about your posture as you walk will tone your arms, shoulders and upper back, it will also help you tone you're abs and if you are doing all of these things correctly reduce your waistline.

It's a double benefit for you and your body you will have a better posture and a little walking workout at the same time.

Avoid looking down at the ground or hunching over with your shoulders and back as you walk. Instead, keep your chin up and look in front of you instead of down.

Keep your core tight and your shoulders down and back. This position helps to strength your muscles, allowing you to have good posture all day long.

TONES MUSCLES AND STRENGTHENS YOUR BONE STRUCTURE:

You need your joints to absolutely work at their best for you to gain all the benefits of walking.

For joints to work to their best capacity they need to be kept moving.

A walking regime will have numerous benefits for you:

- Knee joints will get a regular work out making them stronger and more durable. For healthy joints you need to keep them moving.
- Regular walking increase muscle strength and giving definition to calves, quads, hamstrings and lifting glutes.
- It will keep your bones strong and joints healthier increasing bone density helping to maintain healthy joints. Walking is great exercise for stimulating and strengthening bones too.
- Walking has also been proven to fend off or slow down conditions like arthritis and prevent or at least alleviate back pain.

A BOOST FOR ENERGY LEVELS:

A nice brisk walk gives us the best source of natural energy that we can have.

Our bodies get an increased oxygen supply from a boost in circulation which feeds every single cell in the body giving a feeling of increased alertness and a feeling of being 'alive'.

It can also increase **levels** of cortisol, epinephrine, and norepinephrine. Those are the hormones that help elevate energy levels.

If you regularly feel fatigued a walk is a proven way of boosting energy levels – far better than a nap or a cup of coffee.

We all feel sluggish at times but taking a walk is the perfect remedy.

When you walk your body releases endorphins (you will feel happier), it will help with the quality of your sleep too.

Walking is a wonderful reliever of stress and trains the heart to work a lot more efficiently, getting more oxygen to your organs and brain which affects your mood.

Getting out and about in daylight can boost natural levels of vitamin D, a nutrient that's hard to get from food, but the body synthesiser's by exposure to sunlight – one of the primary sources of natural vitamin D.

Vitamin D is a nutrient that plays a massive role in physiological areas like bone health.

MAINTAIN GOOD BRAIN HEALTH:

As we get older our brains can become a troublesome part of our body

Dementia is the most obvious condition to mention as it affects 1 in 14 people over 65 and 1 in 6 once we reach 80 years old and beyond.

My own mother suffered from dementia and I remember at one appointment her consultant saying to me that if I lived to be 100 years old the chance of getting dementia rises to around 33% or 1 chance in 3.

The really good news is that walking as a form of exercise REDUCES the risk of dementia by up to 40%.

It's been shown that older people who walk 6 miles (9.65 kilometres) or more a week can avoid 'brain shrinkage' which means their memory is preserved for longer.

Walking can help fight off feelings of isolation and loneliness too.

A recent survey by the charity *Mind* found 83 per cent of people with mental health issues looked to and relied upon exercise to help lift their mood.

HELP YOU LOSE WEIGHT:

A rough figure for a person to start losing weight is to burn about 600 calories MORE a day than they eat and drink.

Walking to lose weight will involve faster walks because you can burn off twice as many calories walking at 4miles per hour (around 6.5 kilometres an hour) than you can by walking at a more leisurely 2 miles an hour.

There is one principal reason for this to be the case.

Walking faster increases muscle mass and tone and the more muscle that a person has the faster their metabolism, meaning more calories are burned off.

So, you can't amble and lose weight you will have to go at a slightly increased speed to get the result that you want.

The burning of calories is also determined by height and weight factors for an individual together with the length of walks taken.

As a rule of thumb walking at 3 to 3 and a half mile an hour is considered a healthy walking speed and it is the speed to enjoy all the benefits of walking.

But I'm aware that people have very different levels of fitness and body weight and therefore quite different realistic walking speeds particularly when first starting a *walking for health exercise plan.*

Physical activity that is purposely built into a daily lifestyle plan is one of the best ways to start losing weight and keep the weight off once you have shed those pounds.

You don't have to go gung-ho just make small alterations to your routine at first to start getting the benefits and to increase your fitness levels.

Here's a few suggestions.

- Take the stairs instead of a lift.
- Get off public transport a stop or two before you normally would and walk the rest of the way.
- Don't drive short errands like a visit to the hairdresser or the local shops …walk instead.
- Take your dog for a walk or a neighbour's if you haven't got a four-legged friend.

If you are serious about losing weight and improving your overall health, then you should try and make walking a part of your daily routine.

It doesn't matter what time of day that you walk either just make sure that it fits comfortably into your busy day.

Some people are fine with exercise discipline whilst others find keeping a log of all their activity helps motivate them.

For most people there is very little difference between walking a mile or jogging the same distance.

The amount of energy used is about the same, but walking does take a little bit longer.

A simple way to gauge how you are getting on is to choose the same route for a couple of weeks and time how long it takes you to walk it.

You will find that as you get fitter you will complete the walk faster than when you first started. This is a great motivator because the proof that it is doing you and your body a lot of good is all in your timings!

Walking longer distances and using more energy will be the next natural progression for you as a regular walker.

But, remember that health gains are only achieved as long as you don't push yourself too far. Start off slowly and increase your speed and distance as time goes by.

There will come a time when you feel you are ready to increase the intensity of your walks and here's a few ways that you can do that easily:

- Try and walk up more hills and inclines.
- Have a go at walking quickly as part of your walk- do it in little bursts.
- Use some hand weights to make your arms work harder.
- Increase the distance that you walk.
- Make you walks longer, go from half an hour to 45 minutes and then after a couple of weeks up the walk time to an hour.

Walking is a lower impact weight bearing exercise and can be done for longer periods of time.

I have put together some information in table form to more easily show you what the benefits are for losing weight for different speeds, body types and lengths of walks and very importantly the calories that would be burned.

WALKING CALORIES BURNED BY *WEIGHT* VS *TIME*

The table below is for walking at 3 MPH – a pleasant stroll – this equates to 1 mile walked every 20 minutes.

Find your approximate weight on the left-hand side and then see the calorie burning stats under each time period.

Weight	1min	15 min	30 min	45 min	1 hour	90 mins	2hours
100 lbs	3 cal	40 cal	80 cal	119 cal	159 cal	239 cal	318 cal
120 lbs	3 cal	48 cal	96 cal	143 cal	191 cal	287 cal	382 cal
140 lbs	4 cal	56 cal	112 cal	167 cal	223 cal	335 cal	446 cal
160 lbs	4 cal	64 cal	128 cal	191 cal	255 cal	383 cal	510 cal
180 lbs	5 cal	72 cal	144 cal	215 cal	287 cal	431 cal	574 cal
200 lbs	5 cal	80 cal	159 cal	239 cal	318 cal	477 cal	636 cal
250 lbs	7 cal	100 cal	199 cal	299 cal	398 cal	597 cal	796 cal
300 lbs	8 cal	119 cal	239 cal	358 cal	477 cal	716 cal	954 cal

By increasing the speed of a pleasant stroll to 3.5 mph which equates to around 17 minutes per mile you can see that more calories are burned.

Weight	1min	15 min	30 min	45 min	1 hr	90 min	2hr
100 lbs	3 cal	48 cal	97 cal	145 cal	194 cal	290 cal	387 cal
120 lbs	4 cal	59 cal	118 cal	177 cal	237 cal	355 cal	473 cal
140 lbs	5 cal	69 cal	138 cal	206 cal	275 cal	413 cal	550 cal

160 lbs	5 cal	78 cal	157 cal	235 cal	314 cal	471 cal	628 cal
180 lbs	6 cal	88 cal	176 cal	264 cal	353 cal	529 cal	705 cal
200 lbs	7 cal	98 cal	196 cal	293 cal	391 cal	587 cal	783 cal
250 lbs	8 cal	123 cal	245 cal	368 cal	490 cal	735 cal	980 cal
300 lbs	10 cal	146 cal	292 cal	439 cal	585 cal	877 cal	1170cal

A brisk walking pace is 4mph, approximately 15 minutes per mile, and as you will see your weight is the biggest factor for how many calories that you burn on a walk.

You can see that you burn more calories per minute and cover more distance because of your increased speed.

Weight	1 min	15 min	30 min	45 min	1 hour	90 min	2 hours
100 lbs	4 cal	56 cal	113 cal	169 cal	225 cal	338 cal	450 cal
120 lbs	5 cal	69 cal	138 cal	206 cal	275 cal	413 cal	550 cal
140 lbs	5 cal	80 cal	160 cal	240 cal	320 cal	480 cal	640 cal
160 lbs	6 cal	91 cal	183 cal	274 cal	365 cal	548 cal	730 cal
180 lbs	7 cal	103 cal	205 cal	308 cal	410 cal	615 cal	820 cal
200 lbs	8 cal	114 cal	228 cal	341 cal	455 cal	683 cal	910 cal
250 lbs	10 cal	143 cal	285 cal	428 cal	570 cal	855 cal	1140 cal

300 lbs	11 cal	170 cal	340 cal	510 cal	680 cal	1020 cal	1360 cal

When you get to a speed of 5mph, that's 12 minutes per mile, the calories burnt jump again as you expend more energy.

Weight	1 min	15 min	30 min	45 min	1 hr	90 min	2 hr
100 lbs	6 cal	90 cal	180 cal	270 cal	360 cal	540 cal	720 cal
120 lbs	7 cal	110 cal	220 cal	330 cal	440 cal	660 cal	880 cal
140 lbs	9 cal	128 cal	256 cal	384 cal	512 cal	768 cal	1024 cal
160 lbs	10 cal	146 cal	292 cal	438 cal	584 cal	876 cal	1168 cal
180 lbs	11 cal	164 cal	328 cal	492 cal	656 cal	984 cal	1312 cal
200 lbs	12 cal	182 cal	364 cal	546 cal	728 cal	1092 cal	1456 cal
250 lbs	15 cal	228 cal	456 cal	684 cal	912 cal	1368 cal	1824 cal
300 lbs	18 cal	272 cal	544 cal	816 cal	1088 cal	1632 cal	2176 cal

A fat burning walking pace is what you should aim for whether you are walking to lose weight or build up your fitness.

A brisk walk is good moderate-intensity cardio exercise. The speed of a brisk walk varies from person to person as it is reliant on heart rate, age and overall level of fitness.

This means that a brisk walk can be anywhere from 13 to 20 minutes per mile which is a speed range of 3mph to 4.5mph.

WALKING IMPROVES YOUR BALANCE:

Walking for around 30 minutes a day can improve your balance.

For people who have a more sedentary lifestyle muscles tend to become disproportioned for strength and this can cause problems with balance.

Poor posture is something I have covered but muscle strength imbalances, joint and back pain are all contributors to a person's posture or lack of it.

Poor posture creates bad balance.

The solution to balance problems is a daily walk because the increased blood flow will help with joint and back pain and certainly help preserve an individual's balance.

Lower body strength is what we get from regular walking and it is a critical element if you wish to have optimal balance.

People who are obese or overweight have balance issues because they have excess body fat.

Walking burns off calories, boosting metabolism and improves the body's response to insulin naturally.

All of these logical things help with weight loss.

Your body also makes tiny adaptations in the joints and muscles which improves overall balance.

A good way of checking your balance is to stand on one foot for 40 seconds – if you can do that your balance is fine.

If you can do it for more than 8 seconds with your eyes closed without losing your balance, then that is even better.

Give it a go in conjunction with walking to maintain a healthy balance.

All of these mechanisms assist in weight loss efforts. The body also makes small adaptations in the joints and muscles while walking, which improves balance.

IMPROVE YOUR MEMORY BY WALKING:

Everybody likes to have a sharp memory and a good way to protect it is by walking.

Research has showed that the brains ability to store memories can be increased by short bursts of exercise like walking.

Only 10 minutes of light physical activity is all that is needed to boost help the brain distinguish between similar memories.

Slow walking is pretty effective along with activities like yoga and tai chi.

10 minutes of slow walking has shown that connectivity in the brain is increased meaning the parts of the brain that link memory formation and memory storage increase after a small amount of light exercise.

The genteel pace that is walked is seen as a perfect, simple and effective way of slowing down memory loss and cognitive decline in elderly people or those who have a low level of physical ability.

Scientists at the *University of California* asked 36 healthy volunteers aged in their early 20's to do some light exercise for 10 minutes –approx. 30% of their peak oxygen intake- before testing their memory ability.

To be sure of the results they asked the same volunteers to do a memory test *without* exercising.

There was enhanced communication in the hippocampus –the region of the brain that stores memories- and the cortical brain regions (the home in the brain of vivid recollection of memories) in the people who had exercised.

The participants were shown everyday objects such as broccoli or a picnic basket and later tested using those images and very close variants of them to see how well they remembered those specific images.

Memory recall was better in the people who had exercised as they were more efficient at separating or distinguishing between the different memories.

The scientists concluded that a simple evening stroll would be sufficient to be of benefit to our memory.

Eminent neuroscientist, **Michelle Voss** from the *University of Iowa* said she thought the findings were intriguing. "The brain regions involved here are also the regions that are thought to play a big role in the deterioration of memory with ageing. It would be really exciting to see this type of experiment in older adults".

It is something that the researchers in California are planning to do as their main goal is to try and develop an exercise prescription that can be used by older people who are disabled or have mobility impairments with the aim of helping them stave off cognitive decline.

Interestingly the research team decided to do more short walks themselves and have all found that they are more productive and happier as individuals.

Like anything prevention is half the battle and it appears that a simple slow 10-minute walk really can benefit our memories and our recall.

WANT TO SLEEP BETTER? THEN TAKE A WALK...

So many people seem to struggle from sleep problems and use machines, special pillows, gadgets, self-hypnotism and all sorts methods to try and increase not only the amount of time that they sleep for but the quality of their sleep too.

Walking isn't just good for increasing our energy and awareness levels it can also help promote effective sleep.

Regular exercise such as a daily walk is extremely useful for anyone who suffers from a sleep disorder as it helps the body regulate sleep patterns meaning we get to sleep when we need it and enjoy a deeper sleep.

It's important that in order to promote better sleep walking is done at the right time of day. Evenings are out because a good 30-minute walk would stimulate the body too much making it difficult to relax before sleeping and whilst trying to go to sleep.

A simple regular walk boosts the effects of natural sleep hormones like melatonin and doctors recommend that the optimum time of day to do it is in the morning when daylight is bright, and our natural **circadian rhythm** performs as it should.

Circadian rhythms are physical, mental, and behavioural changes that follow a daily cycle. They respond primarily to light and darkness in an organism's environment.

Sleeping at night and being awake during the day is an example of a light-related circadian rhythm.

A survey of postmenopausal women showed that those who exercised for three-and-a-half hours a week had a much easier time of falling asleep than similar women who chose not to exercise at all.

It's been shown that just by increasing total daily steps by around 2,000 which is roughly a mile in distance for the average person, saw sleep benefits from walking become noticeable for both men and women.

On days where a person walked more than their average number of steps, they had improved sleep quality and length of sleep. So just by upping your daily exercise quota by a little bit makes it more likely that you are likely to sleep better.

More vigorous physical activities like running did not have the same effect on sleep as low-intensity exercises such as walking.

If you are somebody who simply does not have the motivation for intense exercise, then enjoying a less strenuous walk will give you the sleep results that you are perhaps looking for.

Walking provides us with physical well-being and far less stress which to many experts are also very important factors in our ability to enjoy better sleep.

WALKING AND CANCER:

A lot of studies have investigated the benefits of regular walking and its effect on Cancer.

There is a lot of good evidence that regular walking/or physical activity can reduce the risk in 3 types of cancer – bowel, breast cancer after the menopause and womb cancer.

A fairly recent study by the US National Cancer Institute released a report saying that was good reason to believe that walking and other physical activity could play a part in lowering the risk for 13 other types of cancer.

Cancers like liver and lung.

It may come as no surprise that the findings of this report were ceased upon by the media who seemed to infer that the risk of cancer could literally be lowered by having a simple walk in the park.

Not true.

Walking is a great way to keep active and maintain or improve your health with a number of clear benefits, but when it comes to cancer the occasional short walk or cycle ride almost certainly won't make much difference.

You have to be active and KEEP active.

US researchers have found through studying thousands of carefully chosen participants that walking and other leisure time activities showed some evidence for reduced risk for 9 other types of cancer.

Oesophageal (the gullet), Gastric Cardia (the top part of the stomach), Liver, Lung, Kidney, Stomach, Myeloid leukaemia, Head and Neck, Bladder and Myeloma.

Researchers have also found that people who do lots of outdoor walking may be at greater risk of certain other cancers most notably malignant melanoma or skin cancer.

This makes absolute sense because of the skin's exposure to the harmful rays of the Sun underlining the importance of sunscreen, wearing a hat and protective sunglasses in the spring and summer months particularly.

The important thing to take from this section is that whilst a brisk walk won't necessarily prevent 13 types of cancer it certainly won't do you anything but good and if you want to get healthier and fitter a daily walk is a great place to start.

If the thought of going to the Gym brings you out in a cold sweat then walking is a great moderately intense activity which will give your body a feeling or warmth and if you are walking correctly you should feel slightly out of breath.

The UK Government recommends around 2.5 hours a week of intense activity like cycling, dancing, gardening, doing housework and of course walking!

You don't have to do the full 2.5 hours in one go – remember it's all about getting active and doing it *regularly*.

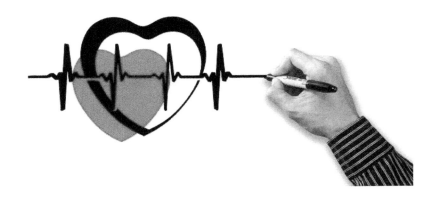

WALKING TO REDUCE THE RISK OF A HEART ATTACK OR STROKE:

Because regular walking is such a good exercise regime to for your body you know that it will reduce blood pressure and help lower your resting heart rate.

Both of these factors play a very significant part in lowering your risk of a stroke or a heart attack.

What is a stroke? A stroke occurs when a bleeding or blocked artery interrupts blood flow to part of the brain.

What is a heart attack? A **heart attack** occurs when an artery supplying your **heart** with blood and oxygen becomes blocked.

Fatty deposits that have built up over time, perhaps due to a poor diet or smoking, form plaque in your **heart's** arteries.

If a plaque ruptures, a blood clot can form and block your arteries, this is a **heart attack**.

Walking to prevent a stroke works equally well in men and women and in doing so it reduces your chances of sudden hospitalisation and can add significantly according to research to your longevity.

Regular walking it is estimated can reduce your risk of death by up to 39% compared to somebody who does no leisure time physical activity at all.

A stroke is a serious concern and the effects of a major stroke can be devastating. Survivors can face extensive rehabilitation and even permanent disability.

Exercise really is like medication and helps your blood vessels to function better and the way that you can protect against a stroke is by protecting yourself from day to day damage of the arterial system in the body.

Recent studies have proved that even a *gentle* walk can help protect people from having a stroke.

And it would appear that there is a direct correlation between lowering the risk of a stroke and the amount of time a person spends walking.

In January of 2014 a study looked at the differences in the risk of having a stroke among men in the UK.

The British Regional Heart Study looked at 3000 men in 24 towns and cities.

All the men were in their 60's and 70's and the studies researchers looked at their walking habits and the status of their health for 11 years.

In that period, 195 suffered a stroke. This amounted to a 6% chance of having a stroke in a 10-year period.

It also turned out that is some men the risk of stroke was even lower.

The study discovered that men who walked an hour a day on most days of the week had just short of a 10% lower chance of having a stroke than those who didn't walk at all or just walked for a few hours a week.

The top walkers in the study, those who walked for around 3 hours a day on average, had a 64% lower risk of a stroke compared to those who walked very little if at all.

It didn't seem to matter too much if they were brisk walkers or just ambled along at their own speed.

The time spent walking was the deciding factor in lowering the risk of a stroke. The longer men walked the lower the risk.

Walking is a really good bet for reducing the chances of having a stroke although it could also be in a combination of a low-stress lifestyle and a good diet BUT walking is proven to help lower the risk of a stroke.

Walking is also beneficial for those whose stroke risk is already higher than average.

A study published in December 2013 in *The Lancet* found that in people at risk of diabetes—and the heart disease that often comes along with it—every additional 2,000 steps (approximately a mile) of daily walking further reduced their stroke risk by 8%.

Walking isn't going to completely protect you from a stroke or a heart attack because other lifestyle factors like smoking, high blood pressure, high cholesterol and consuming too much alcohol are also risk factors.

Making changes in your lifestyle is a good idea and adding walking for stroke and heart attack prevention is a no-brainer.

You can always change your lifestyle no matter what you have done in the past.

To reduce your stroke risk, you DO NOT have to pound the streets for 3 hours a day!

Start slowly and build up your fitness level and distances walked over time.

A rule of thumb according to the vast majority of doctors is try and walk 30 minutes a day consistently.

Your cardiovascular health and fitness will increase in a matter of weeks. You will feel lighter and will be able to walk longer distances without having to take a rest.

WALKING FOR CARDIAC REHABILITATION:

Your doctor's advice should always take priority but there are specific guidelines for using walking for cardiac rehabilitation which will get your heart pumping and your entire cardiovascular system working again promoting ongoing heart health.

As a general rule of thumb most people will be ready to start gentle physical activity approximately 10 days after a heart attack or cardiac event. The key though is to start slowly, try and do it every day but gradually build up your activity levels.

Cardiac rehabilitation programs are very common and have been proven to have a faster and safer recovery with better overall outcomes post heart attack. You will have been assigned to a cardiac rehabilitation team who will give you recommendations and instructions for renewed physical activity.

Walking will be a part of this program.

To get started take a short walk at a slow pace and wherever possible try and walk on level ground. You will know what sort of distance that you can manage it could be a walk to the local shop or a much more modest walk from one room to another at home.

It is a good idea to build up your confidence in the early stages of recovery and you can do this by walking in your garden, indoors, walking a route that is close to your house for example.

Generally, for the first few days of rehab people tend to walk at home or in their garden and as they feel fitter and more confident, they increase their walking distance and the time actually walking by a couple of minutes a day.

Always walk at your own rate that you feel comfortable with as each person is different in the rehab process.

When possible build up to a 10-minute walk and then try and do another one the same day. Gradually aim to walk a little longer each time.

Longer walks of 20 to 30 minutes are a good idea but shorter spells of walking a really good too.

Using a pedometer (a step counter) can help monitor your progress and once you feel that you can walk for 15 minutes without stopping, you can try walking more briskly but if you feel slightly out of breath and uncomfortable then you should stop at once.

Walking at a slower pace at the beginning of your walk is the perfect warm up and doing the same at the end of your walk is the warm down, try and do this as a matter of course.

Your warmup prepares the heart for exercise by only slightly increasing heart rate, it will make you feel slightly breathless and prepare your body and muscles for exercise reducing the chance of injury.

The warm down simply brings your heart rate back down to where it was when you first started.

As you build up your fitness once again try walking on gentle inclines half way through your walk once again only if without much effort you can keep up a steady walking pace and are not uncomfortable short of breath — a little is fine but if it becomes a struggle stop and rest.

Many people find it useful to keep a diary of their progress noting the distance walked, time take to do so and then make a note of how they felt during and after each walk. This is a really good way of charting your rehab progress and a source of valuable and hopefully inspiring information.

Some tips to consider: warm up and warm down before and after your walk, do not walk if your weight has increased by 2 Kg in 1-2 days, if you have any ankle swelling and it increases dramatically do not exercise, if your temperature is raised or you feel unwell do not walk, if you have Angina, always have your GTN spray or tablets with you and finally, be consistent with your walking as the more you do it the more the benefits in your rehab process.

WALK YOURSELF THROUGH THE MENOPAUSE

Before we start this section it's important to recognise the typical symptoms of the menopause.

In no particular order they include: hot flushes; sweating; unpredictable periods; floating anxiety; panic attacks; irritability and moodiness; trouble sleeping; forgetfulness; weight gain; headaches and migraines; aching joints and sore tendons, muscles and feet; breast tenderness; diminished sex drive; vaginal dryness.

The Menopause is a very important transition in the lives of women and physical activity is considered extremely important in tackling some of the symptoms and feeling a whole lot better about themselves.

Walking is right up there at the top of the list of things to consider. You may have heard women talk about how they 'walked through the menopause'.

For mostly healthy women medical professionals recommend moderate aerobic activity for at least 150 minutes a week or vigorous aerobic activity for at least 75 minutes a week.

You have many options including jogging, biking, swimming, water aerobics, strength training, exercises for balance and stability as well as stretching exercises.

But walking is a really good option and in particular brisk walking.

So, why should you consider putting on your walking shoes to help you deal with the menopause?

A brisk walk is free to do and is one of the simplest exercises for menopause that you can do.

It's a great way of burning calories and walking at a brisk pace can also help with mood swings, this is mainly because aerobic exercise really can help fight depression and anxiety which are very common symptoms of the menopause.

Regular brisk walking as a regular exercise can help maintain a healthy weight, relieve stress, improve quality of sleep and by definition your life.

Fitness is very important during the menopause because of these 5 reasons:

- **Prevents excessive weight gain.** During menopause women quite often lose muscle mass and gain fat around the abdomen. Regular moderate intensity exercise can help the fight against putting on weight because it burns calories.
- **Reducing the risk of cancer.** Exercise during and after menopause can help you lose excess weight or maintain a healthy

weight, which might offer protection from various types of cancer, including breast, colon and endometrial cancer.

- **Bone Strengthening.** Exercise slows bone loss after menopause, which can lower the risk of breaks and even osteoporosis.

- **Reduces the risk of other common diseases.** As you have already read walking as an exercise when done regularly can reduce the risk of type 2 diabetes and heart disease. Gaining weight during the menopause is such a common side effect and regular walking can counter these risks and will help you avoid serious medical complications.

- **Boost your mood.** Physically active women have a lower risk of depression and cognitive decline.

Don't just dive into brisk walking make sure that you warm up with some light stretching and exercises before giving it a go.

Time and again studies show that moderate intensity exercise such as walking can help a person battle lots of menopause related issues.

During menopause a lot of women have great difficulty stopping weight gain and worryingly the hormonal changes in the body at this time can give an increased risk of heart disease.

The years of menopause often bring mood changes, loss of energy and depression rates are the highest amongst any age groups.

A 2011 study by the *North American Menopause Society* concluded that moderate-intensity exercise such as brisk walking was a really good mood enhancer for middle aged women rather than much more vigorous exercising.

The study asked its women volunteers to choose a pace of walking that they were comfortable with on a treadmill and then their heart rates were checked to ensure that they were moderately exercising.

The same women were asked to do a bout of more vigorous exercising and were given stringent psychological tests for their mood-state before, during and after exercising both ways.

It was found conclusively that for boosting moods and engendering a feeling of more energy moderate exercising significantly beat the more vigorous one.

The researchers concluded that all midlife women should be encouraged to exercise with a moderate intensity as well as be encouraged to enjoy physical activities that were personally meaningful and that they found enjoyable.

A UK study of over 1 million women over a 9-year period concluded that by exercising two to three times a week reduced the risk of heart disease, stroke and blood clots by nearly a quarter compared to women who were inactive.

It wasn't only walking that was helpful in this regard but other moderately intensive exercising such as cycling, swimming and even gardening!

A really good way of walking regularly during menopause and making it interesting and fun is to get a pedometer. You can buy one or use one of the apps that I mention later on in this book.

Aim for around 6,000 steps a day which for midlife women has been proven to give all the health benefits that I have mentioned already and that includes many of the symptoms of menopause.

As you get fitter and perhaps share a walk with a friend you will find that you will naturally do more steps during each walk which will only increase the 'feel good factor' that this type of exercise is doing for your menopausal body and mind.

THE BENEFITS FOR YOUR MIND & MOODS BY TAKING A WALK

People who exercise regularly often say that they do it because it gives them a big sense of wellbeing.

Many claim that they have more energy, enjoy better sleep, feel that their memory has improved, and just feel more relaxed and positive about their lives and importantly themselves

Walking can be significantly beneficial for your mental health and instead of taking weeks to get results for the physical benefits of walking, mentally the results can be almost immediate.

As you walk your body wakes up and especially your mind. It appears to be a powerful medicine for many common mental health challenges.

When you get fitter, your body gets a lot better at handling oxygen and this helps the body release feel-good hormones called *endorphins* into the bloodstream.

Endorphins are a neurochemical that boosts your mental health, decreases your sensitivity to stress and pain, and can even make you feel euphoric.

Sticking to a consistent walking routine is also a great morale booster.

You will feel proud of yourself when you conquer your daily goal — which, in turn, inspires you to keep going the next day and so on.

There is a little added bonus too -those success-based endorphins that you release through walking will empower you in other areas of your life both personally and professionally.

The mental benefits of this process are helped by the natural high that is generated by your body.

It reduces stress and anxiety and helps to build self-esteem.

Have you ever heard of BDNF?

Don't worry if you haven't but it is a very important by-product of walking regularly.

BDNF or to give it its full name **Brain-Derived Neurotropic Factor** is a protein that is essential for neuronal development and survival, synaptic plasticity and cognitive function in the brain.

BDNF levels are extremely important for brain health and the brisker you walk the more your levels will be where they should be.

Low levels of BDNF are associated with neurodegenerative disorders, such as Alzheimer's disease.

One leading recent study found, walking for 30 minutes at a moderate intensity increased the production of BDNF in the brains of post stroke patients.

Studies have proved that regular walking also helps with sleep issues, reduces fatigue and physically active people have a 30% less chance of developing depression.

A 49-study review by *Kings College in London* found by just walking 20 minutes a day it cuts the risk of developing depression by a third.

Walking is also a great way of helping somebody who is being treated for depression recover.

In older people regular walking improves cognitive function, memory, attention spans, processing speeds in the brain and perhaps most importantly of all seems to reduce the risk of cognitive decline and the onset of dementia.

If you are thinking of taking up regular walking to lose weight, then once the pounds start falling off you will feel in control of your weight and your body image.

The result will be a big boost in self-confidence – a state of mind.

Active people develop a sense of achievement and purpose. Taking a walk gives you a chance to take time out, think and reflect.

As confidence and self-esteem improve, you're also more inclined to reach out and connect with others.

An extensive study undertaken by *Stanford University in the United States* Found that walking increased creative output in the brain by an average of 60%.

I must say I really have had some of my best creative ideas and light-bulb moments when I have been out walking – so it does work!

This type of creativity is called by scientists 'divergent thinking' and this is what walking allows your brain to do.

It will automatically start thought processes to generate creative ideas by exploring as many solutions to the original thought process as possible.

Walking open up the free flow of ideas and is a simple solution if you want to increase your creativity whilst doing physical exercise.

Here's an interesting piece of research that I discovered whilst preparing this book that underlines the point on creativity through walking.

The Journal of Experimental Psychology, Learning, Memory and Cognition administered 'creative thinking' tests to people who were sitting down and people who went walking.

Dr Jampolis of the study, concluded that the walkers thought more creatively than the people sitting down.

Walking for 20-30 minutes day has been proven to increase cognitive function and participants in walking performed better in tests and had a quicker and more accurate reaction time.

Whether you are stuck with a conundrum at work or need a bit of creative inspiration the research shows that it's a good idea to get moving.

Science says that engaging in activities that make it ok for our minds to wander promote a mental state conducive to innovative ideas.

Walking is definitely a mood booster.

Psychologists have found that just a 10-minute walk may be just as good as a 45-minute workout when it comes to relieving anxiety.

After only 12 minutes of walking the brain and your mood are boosted resulting in a more jovial attitude, more vigour, attentiveness and self-confidence compared to the same amount of time being more sedentary.

If you suffer from a tendency to be a negative thinker walking in the countryside or a forest seems to reduce its levels and negative experiences and thoughts can be controlled.

There is part of our brain that deals in negative emotions and walking helps control the influence that it has – negative emotions raise the risk of depression.

If you have a bad day at work or issues that are negatively playing on your mind it may be natural for you to reach for some chocolate or pour yourself a glass of wine to try and help.

Walking is a zero-calorie alternative that offers the same perks and results.

Regular walking is calming because it modifies the nervous system, so much so, that you will notice a decrease in anger and hostility levels.

Once again, walking in more natural surroundings like a park or the countryside will derive the most benefits.

A lot of people like to make their walks social with a friend or a partner which makes them feel more connected through natural interaction and by definition much happier in their mood.

Walking may not make you break a sweat like running or a Pilates class does, but that doesn't mean it's a less effective workout.

Taking a twenty-minute walk around your neighbourhood or in the closest park to where you live or work or opting to walk instead of catching the bus on your way home from work, will keep your brain healthy in the long run.

WALKING TO REDUCE LONELINESS

Poor physical health and mental health often go hand in hand.

It is estimated that 1 in 4 of us will experience some form of mental health problems in our lives.

Looking after our mental health is key and loneliness can be a major factor. It is something that can affect just about anyone and for many people manifests itself in waves throughout a lifetime. It is estimated that between 5% and 18% of adults experience loneliness on a regular basis and it is a fact that it is a state of mind that is a big health risk and has a very negative impact of our mental health.

Loneliness can mutate into depression and it has been proven that exercise and some companionship can really make all the difference.

Many walking clubs are committed to helping people connect, reducing loneliness and a feeling of isolation.

For example, walking and talking and being involved in exercise with others reduces loneliness and benefits mental health.

Being outside in nature or wide open green spaces has been proven time and again to have a very positive impact on mental health just by being closer to greenery and being outdoors in a totally natural environment which also has the added benefits of reducing anxiety, stress and fatigue.

Physically active people have up to a 30% reduced risk of becoming depressed and for those that suffer from bouts of depression walking and staying active will help them recover.

Here's Something a Little More Leisurely for Walking and Boosting Your Mental Health

If you like the sound of all the various mental health benefits of walking but perhaps are not overly enthusiastic at walking at a reasonable brisk pace for an average of 30 minutes a day per week.

Then I'm assuming that if there was a way of expending less physical effort to get a lot of the same benefits that you would be interested.

Something called **'Forest Bathing'** could be the perfect solution.

Put simply 'Forest bathing' is taking time to unwind and connect with nature to improve your health.

Forest bathing is retreating to nature to immerse in the forest atmosphere and the good news is you don't have to live near a forest or travel to one to 'bathe' you can actually practice 'Forest Bathing' under a single tree.

The practice originated in Japan in the 1980's and was named by the Japanese Ministry of Agriculture, Forestry and Fisheries as "Shinrin-yoku," which roughly translated into English means "forest bathing."

It is based on ancient Shinto and Buddhist practices.

In Japan 'forest bathing' was created as a response to a real public health crisis with rising levels of stress levels at work and a very high 'spike' in rates of auto-immune disease.

The practice of 'forest bathing' is designed to let nature into the body through the 5 senses of seeing, hearing, touching, smelling and tasting.

Japan at the time was suffering from mass migration from rural areas to the big cities and its natural forests became uncared for and in many cases 'sick forests'.

Professor Yoshifumi Miyazaki is the author of 'Shinrin-Yoku' – the Japanese way of forest bathing for health & relaxation, and he did some ground-breaking research into 'why we feel relaxed when we encounter nature'.

His first Forest Bathing experiments were carried out on the Island of Yakushima where the professor researched the effects of Cedar trees on the stress hormone levels in the human body.

Professor Dr. Iwao Uehara of the Tokyo University of Agriculture and president of The Society of Forest Amenity & Human Health Promotion in Japan went a step further and formally defined 'Forest Therapy' to the Japanese Forest Society in 1999.

His conclusion was that Shinrin-ryoho (Forest Therapy) was an ideal therapy for people with a disability, suffering from illness, mental health and lifestyle diseases.

It utilises the many healing properties said to be found in forest and trees and can deal very effectively with preventing illness, provide relaxation opportunities and a perfect therapy environment for rehabilitation.

He encourages walking mindfully and exercising in a forest to help change our mindsets and perspectives on life.

Today he continues to promote *Forest Therapy* as a way of making both forest and human beings healthier.

Clearly, embracing a forest in this way is the complete antithesis of a sweaty hike in a forest which is what most of us think of when we take a trip to the woods.

Forest Bathing is done at a much slower pace and is totally focussed on fully experiencing nature and all it has to offer.

It's not about the exercise, getting your heart rate up or ensuring that you cover a set distance. It's a much gentler and mindful form of slow walking based on relaxation and appreciation.

Forest Bathing has numerous other benefits as well.

Multiple forest bathing studies have demonstrated its ability to significantly reduce blood pressure, stress levels and resting pulse rate.

A trip through the woods will also increase your body's *adiponectin levels*. These have an anti-inflammatory effect on blood vessel cells and have been shown to decrease the risk of heart attack.

Increased adiponectin is also inversely related to obesity and insulin resistance.

It is secreted by fat cells and regulates our fat metabolism, glucose levels and propensity to gain weight.

Forest bathing reduces blood glucose levels, even in diabetics.

In a major study, Diabetic patients did a forest bathe walk every eight months for six years.

Even though their time spent forest bathing was very spaced out, their blood glucose levels still showed significant improvement.

Forest bathing also helps what are called *NK cells* or Natural Killer cells.

Natural killer cells are a type of lymphocyte (a white blood **cell**) and a component of innate immune system. **NK cells** play a major role in the host-rejection of both tumours and virally infected **cells.**

The more you have the better it is.

NK cells selectively seek out and destroy cancer cells and bacterial infections in the body. They're also smart enough to target a viral infection inside of one of your cells, without destroying the entire cell.

A Japanese study that involved a three-day camping trip to a forest, saw participants average a massive 50 percent increase in NK cell activity which lasted for a further 30 days.

The trees and plants in the forest emit substances called phytoncides - think of them as wood essential oils - which have been found to boost the immune system.

Qing Li a Japanese scientist who has been carrying out Shinrin yoku (Forest bathing) research for many years, showed that it increases the NK, or Natural Killer cell activity in people, with at least some of this effect coming from phytoncides.

Forest bathing has been scientifically shown to increase immunity, decrease the risk of cancer and help you to recover from illness faster.

In researching this book, I even came across details of a small study where even looking at trees through a hospital window increased recovery time for gallbladder surgery patients.

If you are looking for higher energy levels by day and better sleep by night a little bit of Forest bathing could well be the answer.

Lots of people notice that feeling of revitalisation after taking a deep breath in a natural location.

It isn't our imaginations; Forest bathing has been shown to increase vigour and fight feelings of fatigue.

It also triggers hormones and body processes that help us get improved sleep.

Being in a forest environment can also reduce dopamine and cortisol levels in the body reducing stress and calming the mind.

We'd all agree that mental health issues are very much to the fore and Forest bathing can help in this regard.

A recent small study of just 19 men showed that anxiety, depression and confusion levels significantly reduced after a Forest bathing trip.

These men were compared to another group of men who only walked through an urban area and whilst they had the benefits of outdoor exercise, they did not replicate the results of the Forest bather's in the 3 areas significant to their mental health.

Inflammation relief can also be a benefit of Forest bathing.

The air in forest's is much cleaner than in towns or cities and trees in a forest busily convert carbon dioxide into fresh oxygen for our lungs.

Patients suffering from COPD and asthma have shown lower levels of lung inflammation after Forest bathing because something called D-limonene (a Terpene) which is found naturally in the air of many forests is anti-inflammatory.

Cypress, Fir and Pine trees are Terpene rich.

Terpenes are some of the main anti-inflammatory by-products released by trees into the forest air.

As a result, eczema and psoriasis sufferers have felt reduced symptoms because terpenes have calmed their inflammation.

There are designated 'Forest Bathing' areas in Japan, the UK and the United States to name but a few locations but a quick Google will tell you if there is a Forest bathing area near you.

Although as I mentioned a little while ago if you don't live near a forest or don't have much time then a healthy single tree will still give you the experience and hopefully some of the benefits.

THE DIFFERENT TYPES OF WALKING THAT YOU CAN DO:

Let's face it, we all walk every day, unless we are bed-ridden of course.

But there's a difference between walking from your front door to the garage, walking round to the shops at lunchtime, and the kind of walking you see every 4 years when you watch the Olympics on tv.

One thing that I'm certain of is that there is a 'type' of walking that is suitable for every person in the world.

So, depending on the goals you wish to achieve in looking after your physical and mental health it's important to identify which walking activity is best suited to you.

There are so many different types of walking – some are obvious, and some may surprise you!

First up let's start with a very easy one that you probably do most days anyway. The amble.

AMBLE WALKING:

This type of walking is invariably slow and has no definable end destination.

It's just like when you go to get some lunch or wander around the shops.

An amble has no real purpose; you just go where the mood takes you.

It is completely free to do and as you have read already just because it's a slower paced walk it actually does have some health benefits.

Ambling is a great way to start your new life as a healthy walker because you can increase the times of your ambles every day and build up your overall fitness.

An amble can be 5 minutes or even half an hour – the point is that you are actually doing something physical which your body will like.

Next time you are stuck at your desk and you decide to get out of the office or your workplace as soon as you put one foot in front of the other you are taking an amble.

Walking around indoors counts as ambling too!

CASUAL STROLL WALKING:

This type of walking is a little more energetic that an amble.

How many times have you sat staring at a computer screen for hours and decided that you can't take it anymore and need to get out into the fresh air?

You casually stroll when you have more time on your hands, no must do errands to run and walk at a slightly quicker pace than an amble.

A casual stroll really does let you rest your mind, get some fresh air and start exercising your body.

As much as a lot of people do this on their own and enjoy the solitude of strolling it can also be an opportunity to chat to friends and family on the phone whilst you are doing it.

This is not the type of walking that I mentioned when you can speak but are not able to sing. That type of walking is coming up.

A casual stroll doesn't just have to be for a lunchtime. Many people do it before they go to work or when they get home.

If 'strolling' appeals to you all you have to do is commit to do it on a regular basis to start feeling the physical and mental benefits of being fitter and less stressed.

STEADY WALKING:

Ambling and casual strolling are sort of 'walking lite'.

Steady walking is up a level.

This the beginning of the types of walking that will start to get you a lot fitter.

Steady walking is a faster but manageable pace and you will definitely start to feel that you are doing some exercise.

It's when you go out for a walk with a route in mind and a time frame for your walk like a lunch hour or after work before you travel home.

There are no hard and fast rules you just have to make the time to do it.

A steady walk is around 3 miles per hour, although that is not written in stone, but you should look to cover a mile every 20 minutes or perhaps slightly more.

You don't dawdle but have a clear objective like going to a shop, visiting the bank or picking up some food.

Your mindset is that not of an ambler but as a walker with purpose to get everything that you need to do and that can only be achieved by steady walking.

You will by-pass the amble walkers to achieve your goals because you are going faster than they are.

Steady walking can be done anywhere and is a great way of enjoying the outdoors with a friend or a partner to exercise and chat with whilst you do it.

BRISK WALKING:

The key difference between brisk walking and the previous ways that I have mentioned so far is when you walk briskly you should feel just a little out of breath.

Not gasping for air or struggling physically just walking at a pace that tells your body that a little more is being demanded of it.

The best way to approach a brisk walk is to do a few stretches before you set off so as to avoid any unnecessary injuries.

You should walk at a pace that allows you to talk but not sing – which depending on your singing voice may or may not be a godsend.

The pace should be quicker than a steady walk and one that you should be able to keep up for an hour.

As usual it's best if you commit to a brisk walk on a weekly basis or if you are feeling adventurous maybe every couple of days.

Brisk walking will get your heart rate up and burn calories, so it is a perfect physical activity if you are looking to lose weight.

Some people although keen to get their trainers on and get outside need a little motivation and a great tip is to agree to go for a brisk walk with a friend who you can share the experience and the same goals with.

You will be amazed at how an appointment to walk with someone else will totally focus you and ensure that you don't let them down.

Of course, you could well be disciplined enough to walk on your own which is great but do concentrate on keeping up a steady pace to reap the maximum benefits.

If you are reasonably fit, you should be able to cover 3.5 to 4 miles within an hour by brisk walking and as you get to enjoy walking more and more you will find that the time really does fly.

Always ensure that you wear good footwear and not too many layers of clothes because as soon as you get up to your comfortable pace you will notice that your body will start to feel warm.

Brisk walking also gives you a chance to keep an eye on your blood pressure.

Don't expect instant miracles but by taking your BP before and after your brisk walk you should notice healthier levels after a couple of weeks or so particularly if you walk 3 to 4 times a week.

POWER WALKING:

This is the first all over workout type of walking.

It's similar to brisk walking but a touch quicker because you will be using your arms to propel you that little bit faster.

The body mechanics of power walking are as follows:

You push off on each stride using your toes ensuring that your back leg is straight enough for you to be safe and strong in your movement.

As you move forward you should feel your heel land first and at the same time your back leg will start to lift off from your toes.

You will notice that as you transfer your weight in a forward motion you will start to feel power in your back leg as it pushes off.

In power walking the arms should be like pistons. Your elbows should be at 90 degrees as the arms pump backwards and then forwards.

You use your shoulders to push forward and raise your arm high but make sure that your hand does not go above shoulder level.

Tuck your elbows in and this will give you the feeling that you are punching the air as you walk forward.

A proficient and regular power walker should be walking at 5 miles per hour meaning that they cover a mile in 12 minutes.

Power walking is actually becoming very popular and a lot of people do it as an alternative to jogging which can have detrimental effects on joints and feet.

This type of accelerated walking is a calorie burner too and I have heard it claimed that you will burn off just as many calories by power walking than you would if you were jogging.

Power walking is a great option for anyone on a specific dieting regime who wants to burn calories and lose weight.

RACE WALKING:

Power walkers who get the competitive bug often turn to this type of walking as they pursue the next level of walking fitness and wellbeing.

Race walking is about two things – endurance and speed.

Race walkers are the people who you may have seen on tv who have a side to side wobble when they walk.

Their walking style is highly exaggerated but although funny to some to watch it really is physically very demanding.

If you try it and enjoy it you may get the urge to enter competitions of which there many.

Typical race distances for race walking are 10k,20k and even 50k or sometime more!

The golden rule for any race-walking competitor is always to keep one foot on the ground to not do so will result in a warning or perhaps even worse a disqualification from the competition.

MARATHON WALKING:

I'm sure you have heard of marathon running but maybe not marathon walking.

Marathon walking is becoming a regular addition to Marathon running races in cities like London and New York.

The marathon walk is 26.2 miles just like the distance that it is for the runners and the top walkers can get quite close to 6 hours for their marathon walk.

Less experienced walkers usually do it within 8 hours.

It is all about speed and endurance once again but sometimes the route is slightly different to the one that the runners take.

For example, at a recent London marathon the 'walkers' went a different route that took in lots of film sets in the capital.

The walkers saw where films like Bridget Jones, Harry Potter, Love Actually and some of the Bond films were made.

Marathon walking may be something that you wish to aspire to and it's a lot of fun, very good for you and a different way of spending a day outdoors.

NORDIC WALKING:

As somebody who is married to a Scandinavian this is a type of walking that I know all about.

Nordic Walking is its official name, but many people know it as 'Pole Walking'.

This type of walking came about so that Skiers to keep up their training levels in the off season.

If you have ever been skiing, you will appreciate how much of a workout the sport is for the muscles in the body.

It is the same with Nordic Walking because you hold poles in each hand which you use to push down on so that you get a forward momentum.

The result of this action is using a lot of muscles that you wouldn't ordinarily use doing more regular types of walking exercise.

The poles have to be the exact same length for pretty obvious reasons, and they can be used on soft or hard ground.

It is a common sight in Scandinavia to see many elderly people walking with poles not only for extra stability but also the thorough muscular exercise that Nordic style walking gives them.

SWIMMING POOL WALKING:

Swimming pool walking is amazing for building muscle and for cardio-vascular health.

It is also a pastime that can help people who are in rehabilitation and less mobile really make progress on becoming fitter and healthier.

You don't need to be a swimmer to do it either.

If you have ever tried to run or walk for that matter in a swimming pool, then you will have experienced that it really is hard to move fluidly and quickly in water when you are upright.

Pool walking is an effective, easy to do and learn activity which is performed in waist to shoulder deep water.

You will get the toning that you would from going to the gym and weight training, the heart and circulatory system benefits of fast walking and even aerobics plus the flexibility of a person who does regular Yoga – all from around 30 minutes of pool walking a day.

Water provides resistance to all parts of the body and tones and strengthens all your muscles uniformly in a balanced way.

Every muscle that you use in your legs during normal walking – glutarals, quadriceps, gastrocnemius, hamstrings, anterior tibialis and ankle muscles – all get used in swimming pool walking as well.

Swimming pool walking is not all about muscle building.

It's also about burning calories and strengthening stomach muscles without having to do one sit-up or even worse.

Pool walking does burn calories and fat.

It also helps with your general balance because your body has to react to the water around you by staying buoyant.

Swimming pool walking is not high impact exercise its very low impact and friendly to your joints.

As you hopefully would expect I have done my research on swimming pool walking and this is what I have discovered about the do's and don'ts.

Before you really get going with your walk a good idea is to get into the pool and warm up and a great way to do this is just to walk slowly around the pool for about 5 minutes.

When you feel comfortable and ready to begin your walking start at one end of the pool or at one side and walk at a moderate, comfortable pace across the pool to the other side and back again.

The higher you are out of the water the easier the walking.

The deeper your body goes the harder your walking workout will be.

The more you walk the more that you can vary your pool walking and increase the intensity by starting to move your arms and legs.

If you extend your arms out sideways and keep them underwater with your palms facing forward, then bring your arms towards each other with your fingers closed and cross them in front you will feel resistance and the benefit the resistance is having on your body.

Try swooping both arms from side to side and vary leg movements.

A good exercise I saw a group do was making a 'V' with their legs and stepping 'in out in out' as they made their way across the pool.

Try lifting your knees to your chest alternatively.

Another good exercise is moving up and down on your toes on the spot in the pool and then maybe even try a gentle jog in slightly deeper water.

Once you get used to this form of walking you will come up with your own exercises that you feel are best for you.

In water resistance determines your intensity and as you do more exercise you will feel your heartrate increase. Remember you are in charge so don't overdo it.

The more surface area of your body that is in contact with the water the more the resistance and the harder your exercises will be.

A lot of people like to start off in the water pretty modestly but then suddenly have a spurt of harder aqua exercise and so on.

Always have a cool down after swimming pool walking by staying in the water for a few minutes and relaxing.

You do this to bring your heart rate back to where it was before you started.

Your first aim should be to get used to walking in shallow water and then as you feel stronger and more confident you can try light jogging in the same depth of water or deliberately faster walking.

Swimming pool walking first and foremost will exercise your leg muscles and your groin muscles.

By adding a spring to your step, you will start to exercise your thigh muscles.

TIPS FOR SWIMMING POOL WALKING

1. Most swimming pool walkers wear some type of footwear.

    The bottom of a swimming pool can be uneven and even rough is some areas let alone slippery.

    The amount of strain you put in the soles of your feet whilst walking in a swimming pool is considerable.

    A good 'aqua shoe' with cushioning and lateral support will help protect your limbs, back and knees from any impacts.

    Aqua shoes are widely available and are lightweight and dry very quickly.

2. Try wearing a baggy t shirt or some shorts to increase your drag in the water which means you will be giving yourself a better work out.

3. Always try and keep a pace which you are comfortable with.

    You should be able to speak, if you can't it means that you are pushing yourself too hard.

    Ease off until you feel you have achieved a pace that suits your level of fitness.

4. When you feel more confident incorporate short faster bursts into your water workout.

    Don't worry if you can't keep them up for long but do make a conscious effort to do them.

    Studies have shown that this kind of exercise is really good for your heart and muscles and can even continue burning calories after you have finished your exercise session.

5. Add water weights to your workout to get extra benefit.

If you don't have any or are not interested in buying any then try filling a water bottle or a milk carton with water and use your arms to pump them into the air as you walk in the swimming pool.

DESTINATION WALKING:

This is a really great way of making sure that you walk for your health regularly.

Destination walking is put quite simply, when you identify a destination to walk to in the full knowledge that you are going to have to walk back once you have got there.

Many people use this kind of psychological approach to walking to make sure that they do the recommended 10,000 steps a day that health experts say is what we all should be trying to achieve.

Personally, I am not so sure that it should be a hard and fast rule but to get to 8,000 steps a day would be a good level.

There are so many Apps and step counters that you can use to measure your step walking but more about them later in this book.

Having a specific location, a couple of miles away forces you to double the distance as a destination walker.

It is much easier to destination walk for long distances because there is no turning back.

Once you have walked to your destination, you have to return.

Destinations could be a friend or family members house, a wide-open space, your favourite café (yes you are allowed a treat when you get there!).

Think of locations like a nearby lake, schoolyard, grocery shop (take some bags with you), or cinema within a few miles of your home.

Lots of people do destination walking when they are on holiday but often forget to keep it up when they return.

Try and seriously consider walking instead of driving not only is it good for you but also the environment.

DOG WALKING:

By far this is my favourite type of walking and I do it around 6 days a week.

I love being outdoors with my dog as much as she enjoys being outdoors with me.

The dog owner and the dog both benefit hugely from regular walking.

For the dog there is much needed exercise and stimulation and for the human there are all the physical benefits that I have covered with the added bonus of this type of walking being a massive stress buster.

Make no mistake about it dog walking is recognised as good exercise.

We all know that most dogs always get excited at the prospect of a walk.

They don't care about rain, wind, drizzle and even snow just mention the word "walkies" and their tails start wagging and they are ready for the off.

A lot of dog owners are the same as their four legged friend but in my experience a significant number would prefer to have an extra hour in bed, claim that they are limited for time or have no desire to go out into the elements and certainly that is the case with bad weather.

For a dog walk to be beneficial to you and the dog it has to be a minimum of 30 minutes long and at quite a pace too.

Dogs need exercise to keep them fit, healthy and happy and that should be the mindset of the dog owner too.

According to a study by Dr Mathew Reeves of *Michigan State University* people who own and walk their dog are 34% more likely to hit exercise targets than those who have a dog and rarely take it for a walk.

The study also showed that dog owners tended to be fitter than people who don't have a pet because of the amount of walking exercise they do with their dog.

Dr Reeves says 'Walking is the most accessible form of physical activity available to people.

'So, health campaigns promoting ownership of a dog and dog walking may be a logical way to increase physical activity.'

His study also found that those owners with larger dogs engage in more walking than people with a smaller breed.

Dr Reeves spoke to the *Journal of Physical Activity and Health*: 'Obviously you would expect dog walkers to walk more, but we found people who walked their dog also had higher overall levels of both moderate and vigorous physical activities.

'There appears to be a strong link between owning and walking a dog and achieving higher levels of physical activity, even after accounting for the actual dog walking.'

He also made the very valid point that there are social and human/animal bond aspects of owning a dog that have been shown to have a positive impact on quality of life and positive mental health.

It doesn't matter what time of day you walk your dog or where you choose to go.

It could be a couple of times round the block, a road walk, a walk in a local park or if you are anything like me a nice bit of off-road and pathways walking over fields and through forests.

Walking on paths and roads will allow you to be quite speedy.

Once you go into the countryside fields and woodland can be a little more physically challenging but the benefits you will reap will be significant not only for you but also for your dog.

The following may seem obvious to you and I but from experience they are not to a lot of people who are dog walkers.

The Do's and Don'ts…

- **Always use a lead**. There are places where leads are compulsory and there are places where they are not. Check what the rules are before you go out with your dog.

    Using a lead gives you control over your dog and is polite to dog walkers and people in general.

    Many times, I have come across dog owners who refuse to use a lead and they get agitated if you ask them to put their dog on a lead when you meet them.

    The usual response is "It's ok my dogs fine there's no need for a lead".

Rubbish – any dog can spook another and you as an owner do NOT know their dog is fine and neither does your dog! They are being selfish and ignorant.

Best practice is to use a lead unless you are way away from other people and dog walkers you will avoid any problems.

- **Make sure you have the right footwear for dog walking.**

Badly fitting or inappropriate footwear can be really bad for your feet and muscles.

Walking is a very effective form of exercise, but the wrong type of shoe or boot coupled with a bad walking action (because of your choice of footwear) can cause foot and shin pain, unnecessary blisters and soft tissue muscle injuries.

Believe me your body will soon tell you if you are wearing the wrong sort of footwear.

Your shoes/ boots have to be comfortable and preferably have heel and arch of the foot supports.

Try and take light steps making sure that your heel touches the ground before your toes.

Walking on grass will be of less impact on your body than walking on concrete.

I use 2 different types of footwear – in summer and early autumn walking shoes with full support. They are not cheap but worth every penny and do not damage my body at all.

In winter up until 3 or 4 years ago I used to walk in half – wellington boots from a well know manufacturer.

They were not up to the job, split and leaked water but perhaps most importantly of all had no foot support. I developed lower back problems – not good.

Now I use walking boots with full support, no leaks and have a body that is ache and pain free.

- **Take a ball with you** as it is a very useful distraction for your dog if any unforeseen circumstances arise.

When my dog was a pup and well into her third year, she would be so aware of everything around her. The first sight of another dog, a cyclist or a pedestrian she would be very keen to investigate.

This can be dangerous, but a ball is the perfect distraction.

One of the biggest tips I could give you is making sure your dog loves a ball.

- **Nobody likes a dog owner who doesn't clean up mess**. There really is no excuse.

Take poo bags with you and pick up and safely get rid of your dog mess.

Many poo bags now are bio-degradable too.

- Where I live, we have recently had a person highlighting dog mess that hasn't been cleared up by circling the mess with a fluorescent green spray!

- **Try a training whistle.**

They are cheap to buy and ideal for teaching your dog starting from when it's a small pup that the whistle noise means that you want them to come to you.

A whistle once again will help you avoid trouble.

- **Treat your dog** when they do something that you want them too.

  A handful of small dog biscuits or similar treats is a very useful way of reinforcing to the dog that they have been obedient for you.

  They really are a very useful weapon in distracting a dog that gets excitable pretty easily too.

- **Beware of the power of the sun.**

  Try and use sunscreen on yourself and your dog.

  The sun can cause you skin problems and so always have a small tube with you when you go out for a walk particularly in hot weather.

  Some breeds of dog have exposed skin if you can see it then put sunscreen on them. Some breeds of dogs can get sunstroke just like us humans.

- **Take some water on your walk.**

  Hot weather means that exercise will make you sweat and your body will need more fluid.

  The same is true for your dog.

- You can buy from any good pet store equipment that stores water and a feeder so your dog can drink it easily. Common sense really.

SPEED HEALING WALKING FOR BACK PAIN:

Back pain is absolutely horrible.

But walking can help. Walking enhances back health because it stimulates the brain to release pain-killing endorphins.

These endorphins have been proven to reduce back pain, speed up the healing process, increase strength and flexibility and make you feel better mentally and physically.

Very importantly speed healing walking should prevent recurring back pain issues.

Your trunk, core and lower back muscles all control the stability and movement of your lower back.

From being too sedentary a person can experience a malalignment of the spine.

This will increase pain, muscle weakness, fatigue and the likelihood of injury.

When you go for a walk the health of your back muscles is significantly improved.

Walking helps open up the blood vessels and increases blood flow to the important spinal muscles.

These vessels become constricted without some form of regular exercise.

Physiological toxins are produced by muscles and are flushed out of the body by walking with the added benefit of increased flexibility.

If your back feels stiff all the time it may well be because you have an accumulation of these toxins.

Increased blood flow and reduced levels of toxins help build up strength in your lower back muscles adding to the strength and overall integrity of your lower back.

Walking also increases flexibility in your lower back.

Very little physical activity can cause the muscles and joints in the lower back and hips to stiffen up. In extreme cases it can lead to a curvature of the spine.

Walking will certainly increase your flexibility as it stretches muscles and ligaments in the back, legs and buttocks.

Taking a walk targets specific muscles, such as hamstrings, hip flexor muscles and the spines erector muscles so they become activated and stretched.

Spinal ligaments and tendons increase in flexibility too giving you a much better motion range in the lower back area.

Back in 2005 2 doctors went public with their assertions that walking was good for back pain.

Dr Dave Drake, director of musculoskeletal and sports medicine at Virginia Commonwealth University and Dr Jeff Susman, chair of family medicine at the University of Cincinnati concluded that walking was one of the simplest things that you can do for yourself.

Dr Susman had a warning for back pain sufferers for them to heed "Start out slow and easy and gradually build up speed and distance.

Walk around the block, to the shops and even use a treadmill. Always walk on a flat surface while you are trying to heal because hills force you to lean forward when you walk and strain your lower back. Be prepared for some discomfort at first. It sounds paradoxical, but it's better to work through the pain".

In the case of athletes, walking may not sound the most intense type of activity and it probably won't increase sports performance. But getting up and about and moving will counteract the physically negative effects of sitting down for any period of time.

Too much sitting can cause niggling back injuries meaning decreased speed, tight hamstrings and tight hip flexors.

If you suffer from back pain and experience a shooting pain in your leg(s) or any kind of numbness, then you should seek medical attention.

The same goes for any lingering pain for more than a day or so which could be an indicator of something more serious such as compressed nerves and/or spinal discs.

Here are some simple tips to prevent lower back pain whilst walking:

- Start out modestly and take a 5 to 10 minute walk every day and then increase the time spent walking little by little.
- Posture is very important. Keep your spine naturally curved, relax with your head balanced on the top of your spine – do not lean forward – and relax your shoulders.
- If you feel regular or constant pain, try walking in the shallow end of a swimming pool. The buoyancy of the water could well offer some pain relief to allow you to do some walking exercise.
- Don't dither. Start walking for relief of back pain as soon as you possibly can.

   Walking can give you immediate relief although sometimes it may take a little longer.

   Improving the health of your lower back muscles and tissue means restoring function to normal levels and the end result is it will prevent further pain.

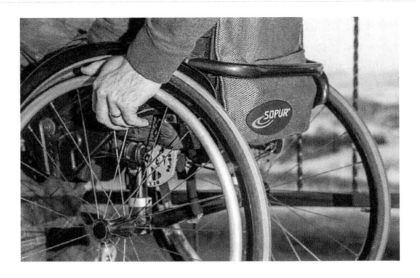

WHEELCHAIR WALKING;

Anybody who is suffering from a mobility disability or perhaps an older person who realises that they may actually need some help to walk may have to opt for a wheelchair to enhance their life.

Wheelchair walking is on the increase and there are many places that it can be done as an outdoor activity.

Mobility is one of the major benefits for a person who uses a wheelchair. Once mobility is affected it is very common for a person to spend more time indoors rather than outdoors.

Physically moving the wheelchair on a walk is excellent exercise as is filling the lungs with fresh air and the therapeutic sounds and smells are good for the mind and overall happiness.

Most wheelchairs are designed to fit into small spaces and to be pretty manoeuvrable allowing a user to move around inside their home and most certainly outside.

Older people often have balance problems and need assistance walking but with a wheelchair there is little fear of being isolated from family and friends.

Using a wheelchair is a great source of help that gives a person back their independence and a free spirit to move around indoors and outdoors as they wish. Enjoying activities, hobbies and the great outdoors.

A wheelchair provides fabulous support for the body encouraging good posture as well as a comfortable seat.

Wheelchair walking gives the user a much more active lifestyle, compliments good health and often results in a happier and more positive outlook on life. It gives a person the chance to socialize, greater mobility, increased confidence and self-esteem.

During my research for this book I discovered a really good website about wheelchair walking which is http://www.walkswithwheelchairs.com/ .

It has been set up by a couple of ladies based in the UK and is very easy to use. You can select individual walks by REGION, DISTANCE, GRADIENT and TERRAIN.

They also ask for visitors to submit recommendations for wheelchair walks so that they can share them with other members.

HOW TO RECOVER FROM LONGER WALKS:

The three things to be on top of for recovery from certainly longer walks are muscle repair, protein and mineral balance.

Muscle repair should be very easy as most people eat the most important factor that aids it…protein.

Protein is the nutrient that is very significant in the growth and repair of tissue in the body.

It is required to help muscles repair but it doesn't mean that you have to devour a steak or drink a couple of protein drinks after you have been out walking, you should have more than enough protein in your body for this to happen unaided.

Here are some examples of protein packed foods – eggs, tuna fish, chicken, salmon, sardines, cheese and red meat.

The protein that these foods contain also helps to promote *glycogen resynthisis* – this is where glucose molecules are added to chains of **glycogen** for storage in the body, another important aspect of walking recovery.

So, if you eat plenty of these foods, your protein needs are also likely to be met.

Foods like cereals, bread, potatoes, porridge, pasta and lentils contain some protein but are also a good source of carbohydrates. These are good because if you exercise for any amount of time you need to eat enough food.

Don't fall into the trap of eating too many sugary and refined foods such as cakes, energy bars, sweets, fizzy drinks etc theses are invariably packed with sugar but very little in the way of protein.

The whole point after walking is to try and replace your glycogen levels.

Glycogen is a multibranched polysaccharide of glucose that serves as a form of energy storage in animals, fungi, and bacteria. ... In skeletal muscle, **glycogen** is found in a low concentration (1–2% of the muscle mass) and the skeletal muscle of an adult weighing 70 kg **stores** roughly 400 grams of **glycogen.**

The balance of water and minerals in your body is damaged or depleted after a long walk or any form of aerobic exercise.

I always consume at least one pint of water as soon as I return from my daily walk.

Think about it if you have been sweating (even lightly) on your walk the mineral and water balance in your body will need repairing.

Drinking plenty of water is a priority. Don't be tempted to eat very salty foods or even take salt tablets which can be dangerous especially if you feel a little dehydrated.

Electrolytes are a collection of minerals such as sodium and potassium, they too also deplete when you sweat but you can easily replace them just by eating normally after you have had an intake of fluid.

Try and have a glass of water to top up your fluid levels and eat a banana which is full of potassium once you have arrived back from your walk and you will not go far wrong.

EQUIPMENT FOR WALKING – THE ESSENTIALS:

You will need to wear clothes that are not too tight so that you can move freely.

Looser clothes also allow your skin to breathe and prevent unnecessary sweating.

Clothes for all weathers are sensible so make sure that you have wet weather clothes, gloves for when it is cold, a good jacket for the winter months and much lighter clothing for the summer and hot weather.

A good pair of sunglasses is always sensible and some sun cream with a decent SPF rating together with a hat.

Depending on the climate where you live you may walk or plan to walk wearing shorts. A note of caution – many places around the world such as Scandinavia, the US and Canada and many parts of Europe are seeing a rise in the amount of ticks in the environment.

Some are fairly harmless, but some are very dangerous and can carry potentially very nasty things.

Lyme disease falls into this category.

It's a fact that more and more people around the globe are getting Lyme disease which can lead to severe neurological problems, constant aching and a general feeling of being constantly run down.

Ticks carrying Lyme disease are clever they can hear you coming and will jump onto you and if you have a dog with you probably, they will prove to be an attractive host too.

Once the tick is on you, and you should be aware that they are often too small to be seen easily by the naked eye, they head for a damp area of the body – they love sweaty areas like armpits / the groin, between the shoulder blades etc.

I can speak from experience having contracted Lyme disease whilst playing golf in Sweden.

If only I had hit the ball straight down the fairway and not into some tick infested forest!

My Lyme disease resulted after a bite between my shoulder blades. I got the classic 'Bullseye' rash after a few days and because I was aware rushed off to see my doctor who sent my blood away to be tested and issued me with some antibiotics immediately.

When my blood results came back it confirmed that I had the lesser of the two types of Lyme disease that most people can get and luckily it cleared up and I had no complications.

I wasn't wearing shorts I was simply wearing trousers and a golf shirt as the weather was warm and muggy – perfect for ticks.

The moral of the story is that anyone can get bitten by a tick and suffer very unpleasant consequences. So, it would make sense to not wear shorts whilst walking in an area known for ticks.

Always check yourself and any companion's - human or animal - after a walk. There are tick removers that you can buy online which are very useful for taking care of them and getting them away from your body as quickly as possible.

Once a tick attaches and burrows itself to your body it starts to begin the infection process after a few days of being undiscovered.

Some countries are far more aware of Lyme disease and how to treat it than others but by being aware you can protect yourself.

FOOTWEAR

By far the most important piece of equipment that you will need to enjoy walking or if you plan to start taking it up as a hobby is footwear.

The obvious choices are walking shoes or walking boots.

They differ slightly and most regular walkers would have a pair of each and rotate them according to the weather conditions and terrain that they plan to walk on.

The most important thing is that they are comfortable because wearing the wrong type of shoe or boot can make you injury prone as well as make the physical act of walking pretty uncomfortable.

Principally, you need to work out what type of shoe/ boot works for you. That means trying a few pairs on, checking out social media groups who post about walking, asking fellow walkers, reading online walking forums and making a note of the makes of footwear that you see people using.

Don't be shy stop and chat to a walker to ask them about their footwear and what they think about them. You will find most people are pretty friendly and happy to help and advise you. Too small and they will cramp your foot, too large and your foot will move, causing blisters as it rubs against the shoe.

For the record my shoes are made by *ECCO technology* (cost around £100 or $125) and my boots are a British make *Karrimor* and you should be able to get a pretty decent pair in the price range of £30- £50 or in $40 - $65.

Both have been a wonderful safe and comfortable addition to my walking equipment, and you will find many similar makes around the globe.

A good walking specialist shop or retailer worth their salt will be able to give you best advice.

If Footwear is too small, they will squeeze and cramp your feet, too large and your foot will move, causing blisters as it rubs against the shoe.

If you have any type of foot, knee or leg issues that might bother you when walking – a good shop will have an in-depth knowledge of why different boots will suit different issues.

You need a shoe or boot that gives you good support, flexibility and a good level of cushioning for the feet. For anyone who suffers from fallen foot arches the support aspect of the footwear is really very important.

Something called *plantar fasciitis* is a very common cause of pain in the foot arches for many walkers and is caused by simple overuse or an injury to the ligament that connects the front of your foot to the heel.

Arch supports in shoes or boots is very important and the foots bones and tendons are significant in distributing your weight correctly as you step forward. If you buy a shoe with little or no arch support, it is quite possible that over time you will experience issues with your feet.

One other thing to consider before deciding on what footwear to use is to decide on what type of walking you are planning on doing over a long period of time.

For simple pavement walking with a dog or a companion training shoes should be fine along with walking shoes if you prefer.

Walking shoes should be fine for walking on grass but once you want to walk on more challenging terrain like long grass, muddy uneven fields and even rocks then walking boots are what you should looking at investing in.

You won't slip as much, and a good boot will give you good support in all areas including arches and ankles.

As you are going to spend a lot of time in your walking boots or shoes it is also important that you get a pair that is the right width for your feet.

If you get a pair that is a little too wide, it will cause your feet to slightly slide around from side to side increasing the possibility of getting painful blisters.

Conversely, shoes that are too narrow will pinch your toes and feet causing some pain as well as blisters.

The right fitting pair of shoes/boots is essential, so take your time trying on as many pairs as you can before settling on your choice.

Leather boots will be stiffer but more water resistant. Leather boots will give you a tougher wear for terrains that are uneven and rocky.

A lot of walking footwear today is made of synthetic material that is much lighter than leather and much more flexible. Synthetic boots and shoes will help your feet breathe more easily and certainly be more suited to walking on grass, pavements and terrain that isn't too wet or challenging.

Wet feet are the scourge of a lot of walkers and most boots are waterproof to varying levels. *Goretex* is a very reliable waterproofing material used in the manufacture of walking footwear and any boot or shoe that has it will usually have GTX after the brand name.

Cleaning and caring for your boots will prevent a loss of waterproofing quality – it is important to look after your newly acquired investment!

One final thing on the subject of walking footwear is the type of heel you can get and the differences between them.

Boots with a heel are pretty good for use on unstable terrain and will give you a much-needed grip when you travel downhill whilst shoes with a flat or slightly curved sole will help you walk better on more normal terrain.

When you have decided on your type of footwear don't forget to walk in them using thicker than normal socks to protect your feet and add some comfort.

SIMPLE WAYS TO KEEP TRACK OF YOUR WALKS & FITNESS PROGRESS:

Whatever type of walking you prefer to do it is fun and interesting to keep track of how far you have walked and for how long.

For anybody walking with the specific aim of doing it to burn calories and lose weight there are a whole myriad of gizmo's and App's that you can use.

Most people have heard of the Fitbit and its variants.

A **Fitbit** is an activity tracker, usually worn on the wrist, which can track the distance you walk, run, swim or cycle, as well as the number of calories you burn and take in.

They are hugely popular as are Pedometers which keep a simple record of the number of steps that you take during a walk or your daily life. Many people use them as motivation for their fitness goals.

Most medical professionals think between 8000 and 10,000 steps a day is a good amount for keeping pretty fit.

10,000 steps equate to approximately 5 miles or 8 Kilometres which for the average walker would take them around 1 hour and 40 minutes to complete BUT if you set a step target like this you don't have to do it all in one go there is no need to put yourself under any unnecessary pressure – walking should be fun and not a route march!

I am not going to list endless ways of measuring a walk as there are so many choices for the technology that you can use.

What I am going to do is share a few ways that I have found to be accurate and most pleasing of all free to use.

As an iPhone user the **Health** inbuilt app is basic and one of my favourites although compared to other measuring methods it can on occasions show slightly reduced readings, but as a rule of thumb it is perfectly fine.

You will see it on your phone screen as this icon:

In the words of Apple themselves "The **Health app** gathers **health** data from your **iPhone**, Apple Watch, and **apps** that you already use, so you can view all your progress in one convenient place. **Health** automatically counts your steps, walking, and running distances. And, if you have an Apple Watch, it automatically tracks your Activity data".

I use it only for steps walked and distance covered, and you can set it to miles or km very easily.

It does lots of other neat things, but we are only concerned with measuring our walking, so we keep to targets. You will however be quite surprised how much walking you do over time and how many steps that you take.

The 'Health' App is free to use.

Next up is my favourite app which has a free version and the more information and data that you want from it will mean you will have to upgrade to a paid version.

Starting out the FREE version really does do the job.

'Map My Walk' is the app and its icon looks like this:

Available as an app for IOS and Android 'Map My Walk' allows you to see the time you spend walking, the distance walked, pace, speed, elevation (measured as flights of stairs!) and even calories burned.

You can set the app to give you audio updates as you walk – usually every mile or kilometre walked, you will also get the time for the unit of distance walked and a split time so you can keep an eye on the pace that you are walking at.

All of these features you can get on the free version of the app.

When you finish a walk 'Map My Walk' allows you to upload and save your workout data and study it either on the app itself or on Map My Walk's website.

A lot of people use it along with friends or family members because it has a social feature that lets you share routes and words of encouragement.

It is also possible to load a route that you have saved (you are given this option at the end of every walk that you do) so that you can use it again, or you can select routes that other Map My Walk app users have done in your locality.

Map My Walk is really as superb service and apart from all the features that I have mentioned it can connect with other wearable technology and apps such as Fitbit, Garmin, MyFitnessPal and Jawbone if you happen to be a user.

To get started all you have to do is download the app, set up your profile and away you go.

Please note, as it currently stands the website is only compatible with Window not a Mac but like anything this can change.

My next walking app that I would like to tell you about is currently only available for IOS users and it's called **'Footpath Route Planner'**.

It's icon in the app store looks like this.

You can download it for free and as with 'Map My Walk' there are paid upgrades for different features like 'Footpath Elite' yearly or monthly.

Footpath Route Planner makes it very easy to map out routes that you would like to walk.

All you have to do is trace a route using your finger on the screen and the app will show you all the trails and roads that you can take to complete your walk.

It measures the distance you will need to travel to complete a walk and the height (if any) that you will have to climb.

The app can work offline too and allows you save and share routes which is a handy feature.

Lastly, a fun walking app called **'World Walking'** available for IOS and Android users.

Its icon looks like this.

I really like the thought process behind this walking app it really is very clever and inspiring.

It was devised by a guy called *Duncan Galbraith* who is a cardiac rehabilitation instructor and basically this app is a constant pedometer, recording every single step that you take every day.

The idea is that you pick famous routes around the world like the Machu Pichu Inca trail in Peru or Lands' end to John O'Groats in the UK or Route 66 in the US, even the Sahara desert, all you have to do is try and take enough steps to complete each route.

The app is really big on social interaction and lets walkers form 'virtual clubs' and work together to complete what are often very long distances.

It's fun! You can literally walk the world.

Features include a facility to manage your walks, update progress on existing ones and checkout any upcoming walk milestones with just a few taps on your phone.

It has a built-in GPS system that automatically tracks the distance that you have walked wherever you go on-the-go.

You can chat and share pictures with fellow group members and discover and join local groups or far-away ones.

Like most apps you can get regular push notifications to keep you right up to date with your chosen group(s) activities wherever you are.

This app is perfect for the walker to be who needs a little more motivation to actually get started with a walking program.

AND FINALLY:

Hopefully you now have all the information and proof that you need to actually start walking for a healthier and happier lifestyle.

Walking is an extraordinary way of getting fit and healthy.

Set yourself modest goals at first and ensure that you stick to your walking plans.

There will be days when you just don't feel like doing it or are super busy and can't see how you can fit in a walk even if it's a short one.

This is where the discipline aspect of walking comes into its own.

Make a commitment, a promise to yourself for whatever reason to start walking.

Sometimes it won't be easy but if you do it the results will be significant.

If you are concerned about safety if you plan on walking alone why not ask a few friends or family members to join you.

To keep walking interesting vary where you walk, pick different routes so that you don't get tired of seeing the same sights every day.

If possible, alternate the time of day that you go for a walk as the world very early in the morning is a lot different to how it is in the middle of the day or in the evening.

Take in and enjoy the sights and sounds of your walk and if you start to feel adventurous get in the car and drive to a beautiful spot on the coast or perhaps a nature reserve or an area of outstanding natural beauty.

Listen to music or a podcast whilst you walk it will certainly take your mind off any physical effort.

Listening to music can also get you into a walking rhythm and help you walk faster to achieve your fitness target and you'll be surprised at how far the time goes when you are walking enjoying your favourite tunes.

Walking is free to do and apart from spending a little money on the right footwear you can get started pretty much straight away wherever you live.

You will find it rewarding, fun, interesting and inspiring because as you get fitter it will become like a must have drug for you. By that I mean that you will look forward to your walks and really feel the benefits that will motivate you to go walking for as long as possible during your life.

I really hope that you get as much out of walking as exercise as I have, and I will leave you with a short article as it was written around the turn of the 19th century on the wonders of walking. It resonated with me and may do for you.

Enjoy!

TRAINING PRACTICE, FAIR WALKING, ETC.

Walking is the most useful and at the same time most abused branch of athletic sports; not so much from the fault of the pedestrians as from the inability or want of courage of the judge or referee to stop the man who, in his eagerness for fame or determination to gain money anyhow, may trespass upon fair walking, and run.

Walking is a succession of steps, not leaps, and with one foot always on the ground.

The term "fair toe and heel" was meant to infer that, as the foot of the back leg left the ground, and before the toes had been lifted, the heel of the foremost foot should be on the ground.

Even this apparently simple rule is broken almost daily, in consequence of the pedestrian performing with a bent and loose knee, in which case the swing of his whole frame when going at any pace will invariably bring both feet off the ground at the same time; and although he is going heel and toe, he is not taking the required succession of steps, but is infringing the great and principal one, of one foot being continually on the ground.

The same fault will be brought on by the pedestrian leaning forward with his body, and thereby leaning his weight on the front foot, which, when any great pace is intended, or the performer begins to be fatigued, first merges into a very short stride, and then into a most undignified trot.

There is no finer sight among the long catalogue of athletic sports, more exhilarating and amusing to the true sportsman, than to see a walking-match carried out to the strict letter of the meaning, each moving with the grandest action of which the human frame is capable, at a pace which the feeble frame and mind is totally unable to comprehend, and must be witnessed to be believed.

To be a good and fair walker, according to the recognized rule among the modern school, the attitude should be upright, or nearly so, with the shoulders well back, and the arms, when in motion, held well up in a bent position, and at every stride swing with the movement of the legs, well across the chest, which should be well thrown out.

The loins should be slack, to give plenty of freedom to the hips, and the leg perfectly straight, thrown out from the hip boldly, directly in front of the body, and allowed to reach the ground with the heel being decidedly the first portion of the foot to meet it.

The movement of the arms, as above directed, will keep the balance of the body, and bring the other leg from the ground, when, the same conduct being pursued, the tyro will have accomplished the principal and most difficult portion of his rudiments.

This will in a very short time become natural to him, and the difficulty will be the infringement of the correct manner. The novice having learned how to walk, and being matched, requires training, which must be under the same rules as have been laid down previously, with the difference, however, that his sweats must be taken at his best walking-pace, the trot by all means being totally barred.

A continued perseverance in the practice of this rule will enable the pedestrian to persevere, notwithstanding all the shin-aches, stitches, and other pains attendant on the proper training for a walking-match, and which every man must undergo before he can be considered worthy of being looked upon as a fast and fair walker.

The tyro must not be discouraged with his first feeble and uncertain attempts if they should not come up to his crude anticipations, but bear in mind that, although the accomplished pedestrian goes through his apportioned task with great apparent ease, he has gone through the rudiments, and that nothing but great practice has enabled him to perform the apparent impossibilities which are successfully overcome almost daily.

Therefore, the young walker must take for his motto "Perseverance," and act up to the same by continued practice. The man training for a match should walk some portion of his distance, if weather permits, daily, in his walking-dress, which should consist of a light elastic shirt, short drawers, and light Oxford ties.

On starting, he must go off at his very best pace, and continue it for at least three hundred yards or a quarter of a mile, by which time he will have begun to blow very freely, and then, getting into a good, long, regular stride, his principal aim must be to keep his legs well in advance of his body.

The rule of getting away fast in trials should be invariably carried out; it prepares the man for a sharp tussle with his opponent for the lead, and will hinder him being taken off his legs in the match.

When tired he can also ease his exertions; but if he is in the habit of going off at a steady gait, in the generality of instances he is virtually defeated in a match before he has commenced racing.

Moreover, he must, when undergoing distress from the pace he has been doing, never by any chance cease his resolute and ding-dong action, for distress, if once given way to by easing, will of course leave the sufferer, but at the same time all speed has also departed, and not for a short space of time either, but sufficiently long for the gamer man, who would not succumb to the inevitable result of continued severe exertion, to obtain such an advantage as would be irrecoverable, as well as to conquer the aches and pains which invariably leave the well-trained pedestrian when the circulation and respiration become equalized--"second wind" it is better known by.

After this happy and enviable stage of affairs has been reached the work becomes mechanical, and the pedestrian from time to time is enabled to put on spurts and dashed that would astonish himself at any other time when not up to thorough concert pitch.

The recovery from these electrifying dashes is almost instantaneous, and the pedestrian keeps on his satisfactory career until sheer fatigue gradually diminishes his speed, although none of the previous aches and pains are present.

The trainer must not forget the previously mentioned rule of stopping the man when good time is not the result of his best and hardest exertions, as that bad time proves unerringly that something must be amiss which requires looking to thoroughly.

As well might the engineer of a locomotive, on finding out that some of the internal works of his engine were out of gear, put on all his steam, and then wonder at the machinery being out of order at a future time of trial.

One word more. Let the man continually bear in mind that "it is the pace that kills," and that slow walking never made a fast race or fast man; let him practice at his best pace, which will daily improve.

The commencement of fast work will most likely bring on pain of the shins, which will be sore after the exertion has been discontinued, as well as other portions of the frame being in the same predicament.

Hand-rubbing with a stimulating embrocation (of which the recipe is appended) before a good fire will in most instances be all that is required, but if obstinate, a hot bath will insure the removal of all the obstinate twitches, etc.

The shoes for match-walking should be of the lightest description commensurate with strength for the distance required.

They should be of sufficient width and length to give the muscles and tendons of the foot full play, without being in the slightest degree cramped.

They should be laced up the front, and care taken that the lace is sound and new.

So much importance is attached to this, that stout wax-ends are now invariably in use.

Some advocate the use of boots; but although stated to be useful if there is any weakness of the ankle--a pedestrian with weak ankles! --is there no cold water?--the heat generated by them would certainly counterbalance the supposed benefit: and there is the difference in the weight, which would tell at the finish of a long match.

DISCLAIMER

This book is about walking and the benefits to the body and mind derived from walking.

To walk regularly and to any degree for physical and mental wellbeing you should be at a certain level of general fitness.

For people who are walking to aid with ailments or particularly to lose weight it is advisable to speak to your medical practitioner to seek the right advice before embarking on regular walks as a means of exercise.

Here are some health issues to consider discussing with your doctor before undertaking any form of walking on a regular basis.

- You're a man older than age 45 or a woman older than age 55.
- You smoke or quit smoking in the past six months.
- You're overweight or obese.
- You have a chronic health condition, such as diabetes, cardiovascular disease or lung disease.
- You have high cholesterol or high blood pressure.
- You've had a heart attack.
- You have a family history of heart-related problems before age 55 in men and age 65 in women
- You feel pain or discomfort in your chest, jaw, neck or arms during activity.
- You become dizzy with exertion.
- You're unsure if you're in good health or you haven't been exercising regularly.

This book is not a medical guide and anyone who walks without seeking a doctor's advice does so at their own risk.

The author and publishers of this book cannot and will not accept responsibility for readers medical issues and always encourage safe responsible and enjoyable exercise.

'How to Walk Yourself Healthy & Happy' 2020 Copyright Zenibo Publishing

No part of this book can be copied or reproduced without the express permission of the publishers with the exception of using relevant sections as part of a bonafide book review.

Printed in Great Britain
by Amazon

87350395R00068